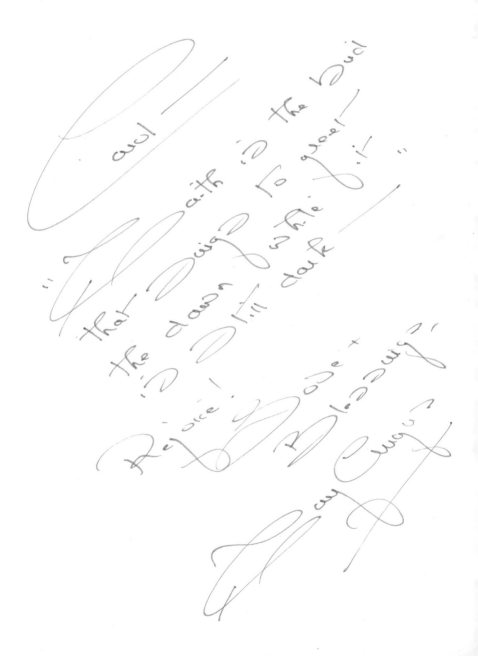

RUNNING AROUND IN
SPIRITUAL CIRCLES

Running Around in Spiritual Circles

FAY ANGUS

1817

Harper & Row, Publishers, San Francisco

Cambridge, Hagerstown, New York, Philadelphia
London, Mexico City, São Paulo, Singapore, Sydney

The author wishes to thank Roy and Ruthie Dyche and Jimmy Breslin and Brennan Manning for permitting their personal family stories to be told.

FIRST EDITION

Designed by Don Hatch
Illustrated by David Marty

Library of Congress Cataloging-in-Publication Data

Angus, Fay.
  Running around in spiritual circles.

  1. Christian life—Anecdotes, facetiae, satire, etc.
I. Title.
BV4501.2.A55   1985   248.4   85-42768
ISBN 0-06-060238-4

---

86 87 88 89 90 RRD 10 9 8 7 6 5 4 3 2 1

Contents

Love reaches for its greatest
joy when it learns to dance with the
wind of heaven. . . . A heart filled with
the love of God, is a heart filled!

Introduction

The question startled me, popping up unexpectedly like the wagging head of a Jack-in-the-box, sprung into action by the trigger finger of a casual conversation.

"How can I find love, happiness, excitement, security and the rest of the ball of wax when all I have to work with is this mortal coil and the coils of the people around about me?"

This book unwinds those mortal coils—it takes a look at just what it is we have to work with. In their unwinding, we find that although fragile and easily twisted out of shape, mortal coils are flexible, resilient, and are made of splendid stuff!

They have built into them the sustaining strength of many God-given virtues, among them, faith, love, friendship, compassion, understanding, courage, hope, and that winsome essence, humor!

Virtues filter through each other like a beam of light dancing different colors through a crystal prism. One virtue draws from all the others—compassion from understanding, courage from hope, and so on. For this reason, through the chapters that follow, there is an overlap as one virtue pulls strength from another.

Their wellspring is the love of God.

When wrapped around the heart of God, mortal

coils become infused with a life-changing vitality that sets us reeling in wonder!

This book celebrates that wonder. It is designed to cheer us up, and cheer us on.

The Gentle Art of Being There

Being there *is love in action*.

A dependable friend is someone who is there to meet us where we're at, to accept us for what we are, and to encourage us to grow into all that we can become ...

Momma Millie is a chest thumper. The chest she thumps is her own. A most ample chest. It is a chest that, through all the expanding or shrinking variables of her more than ample girth, maintains a size or two larger than the rest of her, and holds within its folds a heart with a capacity for living and loving a size or two larger than the rest of us!

She makes of the thumping a personal vendetta, beating a slow staccato rhythm that rises in intensity until it becomes a heavy-handed thud, the pounding of her fist striking short, steady blows as though to beat up and out from the grass roots of her being all that is hidden within the nature of her human nature.

Her thumping culls the senses. Agony or ecstasy, delight or depression, outrage, anger, gratitude, joy ... whatever the emotion, the thumping is the same. She tilts back her head and blinks her eyelids down, like two shades hastily drawn to shut out the blinding brightness of the moment, while strangled gasps of "Oh! Oh! Oh!" gurgle from her throat—an effervescent fizz bottled deep within the confines of her soul suddenly uncorked to surface in popping, bubbly bursts, leaving her always breathless and, more often than not, completely discombobulated.

This is a vital essence of her charm—a willingness to be made vulnerable, to be set awry in the cause of caring and sharing another's life.

I first met Momma Millie, unwittingly, in the long corridor that was the maternity wing of St. Luke's Hospital in Pasadena. Our babies were born there two days apart not only under the auspicious patronage of Luke, the healer, doctor-saint, but under the even more auspicious patronage of the sign of the cross. It was set up high, on the top of a glistening dome, etching a bright symbol of mercy and hope in the California sky.

"What sign were we born under?" my children would ask.

"Why, the sign of the cross," I would smugly say, "the best sign of all!" And I would slip it, like a talisman, into their young lives while my queasy heart whispered, "Keep them there, dear Lord, always under the mercy of your cross."

I met Momma Millie again, this time wittingly, at the annual bake sale of the Episcopal school, adjacent to the quaint cobblestone church that brings a whiff of English countryside into a corner of our small American town.

The rift of time of two days apart was soon bridged when her tot Tom and my little Anne were enrolled in kindergarten there. They were still auspiciously under the cross, but this time it was not on a rooftop but brought down to earth to swing on a cord around the necks of the teaching Sisters of Mary.

She was standing, like a majordomo, behind her own booth of home-baked goodies busily making change from a huge pocket in a floral wrap-around apron. Buns and breads and lemon squares were interspersed with jaunty little packets of homemade mints, pale pink and green, tied at the top with a bit of lace.

"My word!" I said, awed by the variety of her display. "Of all the things that you've got here, which would you recommend as best?"

"Apple-bar cake!" she said, with a snap of finality. "Baked it fresh at four this morning."

No dilly-dallying or coy shilly-shallying. I liked her matter-of-fact, direct response, but four in the morning!

I paid for the cake and asked her to set it aside so that I would not have to lug it from booth to booth. I returned some hours later to pick it up.

"Omigawd!" she gasped, as her lids blinked shut and the banging started, frantically and furiously against her chest. "I sold it again!"

"No matter!" I laughed. "Just bake me another and whenever it's ready, bring it up the hill and we'll both have a cozy cup of tea."

So, grown from the somewhat dubious seeds of two days apart and a twice-sold sale, there came into my life that joy of a friend to plant a memory garden in the soil of my soul and cultivate it through the many climates and seasons of my heart.

Momma Millie has the gift of *being there*.

The virtue of friendship is dependability.

De is the Latin root of "down" and *pendere* "hanging," as in pendant. Dependability means hanging down, supported from above—drawing one's sustenance from a higher source.

Dependability is a virtue, as of God.

A dependable friend is someone who is there when you need them, and still there when you don't.

It is a rare quality.

Dependability is not a condition for friendship. There are no rules for friendship, inasmuch as there are no rules for love. And the two are intertwined. Love often the product of friendship, and friendship always the product of love!

To make rules for love would be to dilute it, like throwing an ice cube into a glass of good wine.

Love is love—it is not conditional or dependent on the fluctuating and/or/if of its performance.

Love stands completely alone, enshrined in the splendor of its own merit, and the joy of love and friendship is caught in the dimension of its multi-hued style. Different strokes for different folks, all blended together to add color and texture to the relationships in our lives.

But undependable friends are friends nonetheless, loved just as much (sometimes more) than those who anchor us with the solid bedrock of their dependability. "The wool of a black sheep is just as warm!"

The humorist-poet Judith Viorst, in her own inimitable witty style, gives us a prime example. Her cousin Elaine, she says, kept her room clean and never "talked fresh" to her mother, while Walter, Elaine's brother, "showed no respect," and the girls that he dated . . . well, "her folks only prayed that he wouldn't come home from infected." In her book *How Did I Get To Be Forty & Other Atrocities*, Viorst writes:

> Elaine, when a card should be sent, sends a card,
> And a birthday is never forgotten.
> (That Walter can't even remember the day
> That his mother was born. Is that rotten?)
> At forty Elaine can look back on a life
> Where she followed the rules to the letter
> And won the esteem of her mother and dad,
> Except—they like Walter much better.

Friends like Walter dazzle us with the sheer outrage of their undependability. They are apt to dash off a Christmas card in the middle of January with neither explanation nor apology, but just the merry message, "Thinking of you darlings!" They leave us waiting indefinitely, grinding our teeth, on a windy corner where they were supposed to pick us up over an hour ago or show up every year and a half, generally on the wrong night, for dinner! They set our tongues clucking and our tempers crackling aglow with righteous indignation, but they also stir the stodge out of us and shake up the smug complacency of our status quo!

However, it is the dependable friends who bring into our lives a series of little miracles. They prove the adage that "sorrow, like a stream, loses itself in many channels—while joy, like a ray of the sun, reflects with a greater ardor and quickness when it rebounds from the breast of a friend."

A dependable friend is someone who is there to meet us where we're at, to accept us for what we are, and to encourage us to grow into all that we can become.

When a lovely, gracious lady named Rosemary Dattolico Breslin died, her husband wrote a tribute that captures the core not only of a woman of great nobility (an aristocrat, as he so rightly calls her), but a woman who had the gift of true, dependable friendship—the inimitable gift of *being there*.

She was a person who regarded life as one long attempt to provide a happy moment or so for another person. Always she was outraged by those who rushed about, shouldering past others, their sides lathered with effort, horses in some cheap race, as they pawed for material success.

She knew that life belonged to those who seek out the weary, sit with the defeated, understand the clumsy and do this not as some duty, but do it with cheerful realization that we are a part of it all.

She thought the word "duty" meant that each day there should be a word or a gesture that would cause someone else to smile over the life about them. Her contempt was reserved for those who would not attempt this. Who are you, she would rail, to go through a day knowing that another day is to follow, and another day after that, knowing that it is all ceaseless, and still refuse to join with us and help soften the path of those about you?

In the crush of the rush that is the rat race (when the only ones winning seem to be the rats!) we find ourselves groping desperately for someone to "soften the path." Those who are there to care and to share.

Momma Millie is there.

Most times she is unobtrusively there.

Like the first day of May. An ordinary day made extraordinary when I trudged down to the garbage cans, a sack full of trash in my arms, and a glint of color flashed jauntily in the corner of my eye. Spring flowers! Homegrown, handpicked, and carefully arranged with streaming pastel ribbons, in a small May basket, set as a crowning glory on the hood ornament of my car.

No card. No card necessary. Momma Millie strikes again!

Suddenly the world took on a glow and it was Camelot in the middle of our driveway. I pranced around, my curlers bobbing, dressing gown gaping, and slippers flapping, singing out of tune at the top of my lungs, "Tra-la, it's May, the lusty month of May . . . the lovely month when everyone goes blissfully astray . . . " Early morning drivers on their way to work, making the curve around the bend in our street, nearly crashed into the bushes at the sight of a disheveled woman, gone daft, waltzing with a sack of trash around a flower-bedecked car . . .

But who cared! Momma Millie had touched the day with a wand of wonder. It was one of those thoughtful gestures "that causes someone else to smile over the life about them." I drove around on my errands with the perky basket wobbling whimsically on the hood of my car. Many smiles, many thumbs up, many paths softened!

A dependable friend is a push when you are stalled.

There are times when Momma Millie is most obtrusively there.

I had spent several days swallowing my tears, nursing a hurt that had me bogged down and gagging on my own self-pity.

"Enough is enough!" she yelled at me over the phone.
"Enough is *not* enough," I blubbered back.

Within the hour she was there, obtrusively on my doorstep a tube of black mascara in her hand. "Go. Into the bathroom. Put it on," she said. "And wear it every day. It will make your eyes look pretty and the sight of mascara streaking down your face will soon stop the tears!"

"Time for mascara?" has now become a password between us, a sure-fire tear buster.

A fable passed down through the years brings the friendship of *being there* into sharp focus.

"Who is a friend like me?" said the shadow to the body. "Do I not follow you wherever you go? Sunlight or moonlight I never forsake you."

"It is true," said the body, "you are with me in sunlight and moonlight, but where are you when neither sun nor moon shines upon me? The true friend is with us in the darkness."

One dark night the phone rang shrill. It's strange how sometimes we can tell by the way that it rings just who is calling—a mysterious telephonic sense.

The familiar voice was somewhat strangled, "I need to walk, *not talk*. Just walk."

Being there is reciprocal. It is not only strong enough to reach down to lift up and give to, but it is strong enough to reach up to pull on and take from.

Momma Millie was waiting for me at the bottom of the hill at the exact point where the sidewalk collides with a bush of night-bloooming jasmine—a lovely scent, heady and heavy. Her hands were tucked into the pockets of a loose-knit shaggy sweater. Her eyes were blazing, large and round, wild with hurt. She set a brisk pace and I scurried beside her, taking three steps to her every two, like the white rabbit trying to catch up with a long-legged Alice, rushing down a dark tunnel the end of which neither could see.

Being there does not need a diagnostic "why" or an analytical "wherefore." Sometimes it is just a silent trudging through the darkness, with heads cast down, a thousand questions left unanswered and spinning against the cadence of barking dogs and night sounds, amplified by the pounding of two hearts beating private thoughts a million miles apart.

Sometimes all that *being there* can do is to pray. Praying is the best thing *being there* can do!

We walked and walked, like two ships breaking a wake into a moonless sea, until our calves ached and at last we sat down to rest on the curbstone—a couple of derelicts, feet in the gutter, heads bent exhausted over folded arms.

After running through several lifetimes in my mind's eye, when I despaired that we might be sitting there forever, Momma Millie looked up—quizzically, expectantly, searching and scanning the night sky as though suddenly touched by a falling star.

She gave a shudder. "My bottom's cold. Let's go home."

More silent trudging until we reached her door. With eyes calmer now, more in control, she turned, said simply, "Thanks, friend," and went in. I will never know the reason for her call that night. But then love does not need reasons. *Being there* is enough.

Albert Schweitzer, the doctor who spent so much of his life setting up a hospital in the jungle of equatorial Africa, said that when we walk together in the darkness the light we have within ourselves shines forth to brighten up the path. We get to know each other "without needing to pass our hands over each other's faces, or to intrude in each other's hearts."

Being there is love in action.

It is not only the heartbeat of love and friendship, it is the heartbeat of the hearth and home.

In the middle of the hard-nosed journalism that finds its way onto the editorial page of the *Los Angeles Times* (often face to face with the stabbing barbs of a political cartoon) frequently is found a piece of tenderness to match, if not better, sermons preached from many pulpits. Letters to the editors of large city newspapers reflect a potpourri of the best of us and the worst of us. This father's letter was the very best of us.

When his daughter was thirteen years old she suddenly changed. She became hostile and rebellious and in the course of the next three years she went on a rampage. She was expelled from high school, ran away from home twice (once she was gone for as long as a month without letting her parents know where she was), was arrested for burglary, and spent some time in Juvenile Hall.

During that period of her life, her father was at a total loss as to how to deal with her. In his letter to the Los Angeles Times (11/10/84) he wrote:

However, I knew that, reprehensible as they were, her actions were not the "real" her. All I did was continue to love her. This doesn't mean that I condoned her behavior or made excuses for her. When I picked her up from police stations in the middle of the night, I treated her with sympathy and respect, for I knew her self-condemnation was sufficient. I wrote to her in Juvenile Hall advising her that the only way she was going to get the "freedom" she so desperately wanted was to abide by society's rules. The one thing we did not do was to give up on her or reject her.

After she was released on probation, her father took her to work with him and paid her for helping out. He sent her to counseling and, as she was interested in art, he enrolled her in art school instead of sending her back to the pressure of her peers in high school.

He acted out his love by *being there*, walking beside her rather than pushing against her. By the time she was seventeen, she had made a complete reversal and was reintegrated as a happy member of the family. That father still gets birthday cards and Father's Day cards that say, "Thanks for sticking with me, Dad."

He had the art of *gently being there*.

He was *gently* there, without critique, in the middle of the night to pick her up from the police station. He was *gently* there, without condemnation, to write and encourage her during her stay in Juvenile Hall. He was *gently* there, without resentment, to bring her home again.

All his personal anguish and distress at her performance was covered by his love for her, and he exercised that love by *gently being there*.

His daughter is now thirty-five. She works as a designer and he says she is raising her own three teenage daughters with love and understanding . . . and I hope his *gentle art of being there*.

Trauma demands love's *being there*.

In a personal encounter tragedy brushed up against

me to forever change my life when a sweet Christian woman with whom I had shared a luncheon and in whose church I had spoken was brutally murdered by her own son. The news made sensational, tragic national headlines.

When the young man was arraigned before the judge, his father stood with him, his arm around the shoulders of his son. His heart was broken, but his love was greater than his broken heart and . . . he was there. Most visibly, unashamedly there. Most comfortingly there.

I have put myself in that father's place a thousand times. I have tried to feel his feelings and reach for the grace that is the sustaining power of his spirit. I have asked myself countless times "could I be there . . . ?"

To me that man is more than saint; he is a reflection of divinity. If ever I needed an image of the fatherhood of God, I found it in that fleeting moment.

When all our chips are down, and we are caught by the horror of our own madness, God—our Father God—is there! His arm of forgiveness, compassion, and grace is draped around our lives.

God's love is always greater than our broken hearts.

With dependability as the virtue of friendship, the value of friendship, then, is built on trust. Its greatest vice is violation of that trust.

Trust has to be earned. Time is its most vital test.

It begins with little things—innuendos, flippancies—and those stretch points that trip over each other in reaching for a mutual confidence to tie two hearts together.

To trust is to risk. To place all the frailties and vulnerabilities of self-revelation in the hands of another who could suddenly turn against us and use them to hurt us is total risk.

Yet Ralph Waldo Emerson tells us that the glory of having a friend is not the outstretched hand, kindly smile, or joy of companionship (important as they all may be), but it is the spiritual inspiration that comes when we discover that someone else believes in us and is willing to trust us with their friendship.

So risk we must.

We are programmed to *be there* for each other.

Solomon, who wrote the book of Eccelsiastes, tells us "Two are better than one. . . . For if they fall, the one will lift the other up . . . if we are alone when we fall, who shall lift us up?" (Eccles. 4:9–10).

He goes on to say that one shall prevail, two shall withstand and a threefold cord is not easily broken.

How often I have called together two of my friends to bind ourselves in prayer under the promise of the threefold cord. I think this is what Jesus meant when he gave us the added dimension of the power of his presence in the "two or three" gathered together in his name.

One reason we have difficulty in reaching out to trust and believe in someone else is that we have become the victims of the abrasions of our past betrayals: "Once burned *your* fault, twice burned *my* fault!"

We bounce these up against the lack of confidence in our own trustworthiness: "I would not want to trust anyone who would trust in me!"

Self-disclosure violated puckers our trust. We

deflect our feelings and throw up a screen to shield our emotional transparency, so that we become self-enclosed—we can look out, but no one can look in.

A party of the first part confides in a party of the second part, but violation of trust begins when the party of the second part says to a party of the third part, "I should not be telling you this, but . . . " After several other parties of several other parts, the word eventually gets back to the party of the first part (whose trust has been violated). Betrayed, she says, "How could she?" and it all ends up with a series of broken friendships. End of the party.

Having been the party of the first part, second part, and third part, all at one time or another, I know.

When in our weakness we betray a trust, we can hear the cock crow in our lives—like Peter—and we weep bitterly.

Now I settle for not being a party to the party. When someone comes up to me and says, "I should not be telling you this, but—" I stop them dead in their tracks and say, "Please don't."

Trust has a two-way tension. There are times when in the anguish of our anxiety to throw off a burden we are unable to carry alone, we are indiscriminate in thrusting the confidence of that burden onto a back that is simply not strong enough to bear it and gets fractured by the sheer weight of it all. In a sense, we then are the ones responsible for any violation of our own trust.

If someone with a breaking back comes up to me and says, "There is something that I can no longer continue to carry alone. It is a confidence that is eating into my soul and destroying my peace of mind. I need desperately to share it with someone else. Will you be that trusted someone?" I try first of all to refer the person back to the party of the first part, the source of the confidence, but if that is not possible, then, yes, I may be willing to become a party of the third part, but the party stops there.

The vow of the confessional is as unto death.

One of the greatest gifts we can offer another person is *being there* to hold their heart in trust.

Another is *being there* to put our hand in theirs and say, "I believe in you!"

It costs.

Sometimes it costs plenty.

Platitudes come cheap—practicalities don't.

She had a bluish tinge around her eyes, a transparency that gave a pallor to her skin and faded her pale eyes into a ghostly nothingness. Looking into them was like looking into the hollowed out eyes of a marble statue—they reflected life only when approached from a certain angle. The light of her body was not in her eyes. It was instead, in a dimple that set itself smack in the middle of her chin. It was an impudent dimple, in a large determined chin—much too large for an elfin face with nothing eyes.

She owned the small gift shop I constantly popped in and out of for a card here or trinket there. Over one winter season when finances were low and expenses high, she took "on consignment" the little plastic kewpie dolls I dressed in hand-knitted outfits. It made us a profit, split down the middle, of four dollars and fifty cents per doll. Times were tough for me then . . . and she was there.

She was there for many people when times were tough.

On the back of her toilet tank she had a large bottle filled to various levels with dimes, quarters, and the odd dollar bill. It had a gingham bow and a label that read, "If you have, give. If you need, take."

There were many who came out of that bathroom with a smile on their face (some of whom she deliberately sent in with a thrust of her determined chin.)

Now times were tough for her. The bottle had long been empty.

I missed her the moment I stepped into the store. She was usually bustling about, shuffling a rack of cards or flicking a duster through china ornaments on glass shelves, arranging and rearranging. She was a "make work"—seldom relaxed, wirey and twig thin.

"Gladys?" I called through the curtain that sectioned off a small rest area in the back of the store. Muffled sobs punctuated the Muzak coming through the sound system, an alien harmony synchronizing pathos into lilting familiar melodies. I sat with her on the small daybed and held both her hands.

"I don't know how I could have ever let myself get into this mess," she stammered. "I've heard of this happening to other people, but, no, it could never happen to me!"

She was overdrawn by nearly two thousand dollars. She had been, for several months. She could not pay her rent or other bills, and she was backed into a corner like a small animal facing that unrelenting carnivorous beast—bankruptcy.

"I've prayed and prayed and prayed," she said. "The people I do business with, they are praying people, and they have prayed with me. Jesus is here but the money isn't."

Then came the slammer.

"Fay, can you lend me some money?"

(Why was I still holding those slender hands? A thousand no's contracted every pore, constricted every nerve. Lent money—ruined friendship. Not much money to lend. Strict policy—never lend money. If the bank would not extend her credit, foolish, foolish me if I were to do so!)

"There's no one else," she said. "I don't blame them. If I were them, I would not believe in me either!"

"Gladys, *I* believe in you!"

(How could I be saying this? Why had I gone into the store that morning? Stupid, stupid me!)

"I don't have much money in my account, maybe around four hundred dollars, but that would help!"

Risk.

Cost.

"No," the determined chin quivered, "I need so much more than that. I guess I'm all washed up."

"Never!" I said, as I pressed the check into her hands. "Here. Go talk to the bank. Gladys, I believe in you!"

The eyes were still a hollow nothingness, but the determined chin came up and set itself at a cocky angle.

She lasted two more months. Then she closed her store.

Bit by bit she returned every cent of the four

hundred dollars. She did not have to; I was made willing to give and not to count the cost.

But she returned to me a lifetime more than money.

On the top of our toilet tank now stands the "Gladys bottle." "IF YOU HAVE, GIVE. IF YOU NEED, TAKE."

The gentle art of being there.

How to Develop a Strategic Vocabulary

The gift of an open ear and a listening, sensitive heart is one of the greatest gifts of love and friendship. It is like that of the ear and heart of God.

As an emotional translator of brash words, generally coming through mouths put into drive before thoughts have been shifted into gear a woman spends an entire lifetime coping with family linguistics the likes of which are comparable only to those of the Tower of Babel.

She is generally married to a man of many calculating thoughts and a few choice words. The thoughts he calculates are the batting average of Steve Garvey, the statistics of the NFL/AFL, and, now and then, the balance in his pension fund. His few choice words may be boiled down to "What's for dinner?" "Can't you shut them up?" and "Aren't you ready yet?"

Conversely, her kids are a brood of many calculating words and a few choice thoughts, the calculating words being, "Can you lend me ten bucks?" and the few choice thoughts revolving around the choices offered by Levi Strauss, Izod, and MTV.

For the most part, she is trapped not only in the gender gap and the generation gap, but right in the middle of the war zone of the communications gap, the peace treaty of which she is expected to mediate and negotiate with all the aplomb of a seasoned diplomat.

She finds herself turning to the children and saying, "Now-now dear, Dad didn't mean to say that. What he really meant to say was . . . ," all the while giving Dad a knowing look and a nudge under the table to emphasize the point. In response Dad snarls (as he rubs his shins), "I meant precisely *that*, and just to prove it, I'll say it again!" And he does.

Then she finds herself turning to Dad and saying, "Now-now dear, calm down, you didn't really hear what you thought you heard. What Janie meant to say was . . . ," all the while giving Janie a knowing look and a nudge under the table. In response Janie screws up her eyes and makes a rude face accompanied by an even ruder gesture (body language), which has Dad reaching for the strap.

All of this takes place under a sign attached to the refrigerator by a magnet in the shape of an Icthus that reads, "May the words of my mouth and the meditations of my heart be acceptable in thy sight, O Lord."

However acceptable the words of our mouth may be in the sight of the Lord, the nitty-gritty is that to the person to whom they are addressed they had best not always reflect the meditations of our hearts—unless of course we choose to clean up the meditations of our hearts.

The light of the body is in the eye, but balance is in the ear. An ear infection can so severely throw the body off balance that we teeter about, tripping over things with an inflamed sense of equilibrium that has us struggling to keep from falling down.

In a similar sense we are balanced or thrown off balance by the words we hear.

What we do most in life is listen.

We listen to the verbal messages that come crowding in on us at the rate of about three thousand words per minute (both consciously and subconsciously) and we also listen to nonverbal messages that range from the innuendos of expression, to tone and gesture, to raised eyebrows and that barely discernible but highly important twitch at the corner of a mouth or glint in an eye. Indeed, research tells us that nonverbal messages carry more impact than verbal ones, and when the two are in conflict with each other, it is the nonverbal ones that are dominant.

In public debate, for example, this is used as a strategy to distract the attention and concentration of the audience at a crucial point in the argument of the opposition. The nonverbal message of shifting one's position, crossing or uncrossing one's legs, shuffling papers, or simply nodding one's head is most effective.

Winston Churchill was a master at this. During one session of Parliament when an opponent was at the rostrum delivering his speech, Churchill constantly shook his head in violent disagreement, successfully distracting the attention of the members of the House. His infuriated opponent finally paused, stared at the Prime Minister and said, "I wish to remind the Right Honorable friend that I am only expressing my own opinion." Churchill shot back, "And I wish to remind the speaker that I am only shaking my own head!"

Our earliest communication skills begin with listening. Then, from the words we hear, we learn how to speak.

But studies show that most of us as we grow older listen on a level of only about twenty-five percent efficiency. The answer to the question of whether two people listening to the same thing *hear* the same thing is "not often enough!"

We tend to listen *offensively, defensively,* or *selectively.* Until we learn to listen *sensitively,* we do not really hear.

The *offensive* listener jumps to assumptions and premature conclusions. This can make for disastrous results. A woman in the office approached the man standing behind a machine and asked, "How does this thing work?" "Simple," said the man, taking the hefty report she was carrying and putting it through the document shredder. "How many copies does it make?" asked the woman.

Offensive listeners constantly interrupt and interject, not only cutting the other person off, but frequently cutting them down as well. With only half an ear cocked to the speaker, they are generally far more interested in what they themselves are going to say than in hearing what is being said to them. Unless they can get their word in edgewise, their attention wanders and they become disinterested and "turned off." They barely listen at all. Hearing . . . they do not hear.

Defensive listeners personalize everything that is being said and interpret it as a threat to their status. They struggle through a conversation with their guard up in order to defend what they feel may be an assault on their opinion, their personality, or their performance. They react rather than respond, push away rather than pull toward, and what they think they hear is usually quite distorted from what is actually being said.

Selective listeners sort, sift, and red-tag. They shuffle a conversation like a deck of cards, pulling out a trick here or a trump there, and discard or ignore what is of little or no interest to them. Pity. They could be learning much, even if it is only a little patience and tolerance.

To be ignored is probably one of the most frustrating and hurtful things that can happen to us.

During my school days a disciplinary measure was to be "put in Coventry." This meant no one was to speak to the culprit or listen to her. If she spoke, others were to ignore her and move away; she was to be completely crowded out. The emotional pain was intense, and I learned then how desperately we need to speak and to be heard.

The gift of an open ear and a listening, sensitive heart is one of the greatest gifts of love and friendship. It is like that of the ear and heart of God.

When we get ourselves out of the way, push our preconceptions aside, and concentrate instead on the other person and their need to say what they are saying, when we become fascinated with the unique individuality and perspective of those we interface (agreeable or not), when we maintain a caring attitude that helps them to communicate, then we truly begin to listen and to hear with a sensitive ear.

A friend of mine has the priceless gift of a sensitive, listening ear. For several years now she has extended it to a young man who developed a severe problem in communication. He has a brilliant mind and is a talented artist. After a devastating illness he became mentally confused. He sometimes phones her at outrageous hours. Occasionally he is lucid, most of the time he is not. He tends to ramble on about airplanes fueled by LSD, chalk people, bright visions, or dark and dismal fears, and my friend listens . . .

"Draw me a picture of what you are telling me," she will frequently say, using his artistic talent as a resource to help get his message across. The picture is drawn and sent along in the mail. Sometimes it is a lovely picture, sometimes just a tangle of lines and squiggles. Either way, it is received and once again the message is heard and answered with a caring note. She takes the fractured pieces of his muddled conversations and puts them together with encouragement and love. She not only listens, but she hears a voice that desperately needs a listening ear.

"Hear through my ears, Lord," she prays. And he does.

Several years ago a popular ditty made the rounds at Harvard University in Boston:

Here's to the city of Boston,
The home of the bean and the cod,
Where the Lowells speak only to Cabots
And the Cabots speak only to God.

A pithy reply came from a professor at Yale University in nearby New Haven:

Here's to the town of New Haven,
The home of the truth and the light,

Where God speaks to Jones in the very same tones
He uses to Hadley and Dwight.

Not only does God speak to all of us in the very
same tones, but he listens and listens eagerly and
equally to the varying tones in which we all speak
to him. From the barely audible, hesitant subtone, to
the highly polished articulate pitch he bends his ear
in cherished understanding and love and says, "Tell
me. Tell me all about it."

God not only expects us to listen to each other with
a caring sensitive heart, but he also expects us to
listen to him with attentive sensitivity.

Henry Wadsworth Longfellow writes of the need for
an inward stillness—"That perfect silence where the
lips and heart are still, and we no longer entertain
our own imperfect thoughts and vain opinions. . . . But God alone speaks in us, and we wait in
singleness of heart." We wait to hear the voice of
God.

In his devotional book *Quiet Thoughts on Prayer*,
S. D. Gordon tells the story of an artist who invited
a friend to come and see one of the paintings he had
just completed. The friend went to the artist's home
and was met by an assistant and taken into a darkened room where he was asked to wait. After some
fifteen minutes or so the artist came in and greeted
his friend and led him up to the studio where he did
his work.

"I suppose you thought it queer to be left in that
dark room for so long," the artist said.

"Yes," replied the friend, "I did."

"Well," said the artist, "I knew that if you came

into my studio with the glare of the street in your eyes you could not appreciate the fine coloring of the picture. So I left you in the dark room till the glare had gone out of your eyes."

We tend to rush into the presence of God with not only the glare of the street still in our eyes, but the noises of the hustle and bustle of our lives still pounding in our heads. We all could use that artist's darkened room . . . a holding tank where we cloak ourselves in silence and empty out our hearts of all our "own imperfect thoughts and vain opinions." Then in the quiet stillness . . . we listen for the voice of God.

Jesus regularly drew himself apart to a place of solitude. He generally chose the desert, that place of perfect stillness, or the slope of a hillside, or grove of trees. And he went in the quiet of the early morning hours, or late at night when the active sounds of a busy earth were muted and hushed. There we picture him listening intensely to the voice of his Father and sharing that sweet interchange of prayer.

There is a fellowship in the community where I live that has set aside the second Saturday in each month as a "Quiet Day." Anyone who wants to come to the church is welcome, and it provides a place to shut out the world and come before the Lord in a spirit of stillness . . . to listen for his voice and his voice only and to meditate over selected passages of Scripture.

When we meditate on the Scriptures, turning just a few verses at a time over and over in our mind and heart, they come alive with new meaning. Suddenly our ears of understanding open to hear the voice of God!

There are external solitudes, set places and times to be apart, as in the holding tank of a darkened room, but there are also internal solitudes, that place we cultivate deep within ourselves that becomes the sanctuary of our spirit, a place of quiet refuge where we can be alone even in the middle of a noisy crowd.

This "inner chamber" we carry always with us. We can go there, shut the door on the glare of the world, and in that private silence speak to God and listen for his voice . . .

If listening is what we do most in life, then talking is probably what we do second most in life!

Words are our most valued possession.

A fascinating study of words placed strategically and effectively together comes from an idiom in the Chinese language, which has some seventy thousand characters—of which even the most gifted of students seldom masters more than ten thousand (and we think we have trouble teaching our kids the art of stringing together the twenty-six letters of the alphabet!). The Chinese character for the word "happiness" is comprised of the symbols for "all that a man has, laid on the altar of God." Broken down into segments, "all that a man has" has as its first and foremost component "the words of his mouth." Another component, a small square, cross-hatched to indicate a rice paddy, symbolizes the rest of his possessions all lumped together.

The Chinese priority that sets words as the primary possession in reaching for happiness is a concept we would do well to grasp.

The Bible tells us that the most vital and yet the most difficult thing to master is our words.

It is not so much what goes in one ear and comes out the other that bothers us, it is what goes in one ear, gets garbled in the process, and then comes out the mouth!

A paraphrase of James 3:2–18 reads:

We all make mistakes. If we can control our tongue, it proves we have control over ourselves. Even as a small bit can guide a large horse, a tiny rudder steer a huge ship, and a small spark set off an enormous forest fire, a word can be used as either a blessing or a curse.

Our words can cause destruction and disaster, or they can be used for praise and appreciation. The wisdom of heaven is pure, gentle, peace-loving, and courteous. It allows for discussion and is willing to yield to others. It is full of mercy and good deeds. It is wholehearted, straightforward, and sincere.

During Vacation Bible School one summer, the emphasis of one of the sessions was on gossip. I gave giant bottles of bubble mix to several college students and asked them to hide in the balcony of the church. On a given cue, they blew thousands of bubbles down on the children assembled in the sanctuary. "These are the words you speak," I told the kids. "Now see if you can gather them up and put them back in the bottles!"

Once said, a word is almost impossible to retract.

There are words that hurt and words that heal.

Deans of college students must have a special place reserved for them in heaven! I learned a valued word from such a dean and moved from "hurt" to "heal" . . .

We were talking about one of the students on campus. She had a peculiar manner about her and was

generally described as "kooky," "weird," "eccentric,"
"awkward," or "odd."

"She is highly *stylized*," said the dean.

Stylized! A good word. An intriguing word. A positive, "pull-me-up," instead of "tear-me-down" word. A very strategic word!

I now no longer think of people as "kooky," "weird," "eccentric," "awkward," or "odd"—only highly *stylized*. After all, in one sense or another, we all are "stylized!"

There are words that work and words that don't.

Mark Twain said that the difference between the right word and the almost-right word is like the difference between lightning and the lightning bug.

For example, reading through the first set of word options in the following description, one finds a totally different person from the same woman in the second set of word options: "She is a woman of firm/stubborn convictions/prejudices with the courage/gall to speak out/mouth off about them. She is famous/notorious for her outgoing/interfering nature and her relaxed/dull dinner parties."

Politicians know the power of words. They hire strategists for the sole purpose of putting together words that work to present the candidate in the best possible image and to keep from blurring that image by use of the wrong words. A classic comes from the upbeat concession statement of a candidate who ran for election in a two-man primary and lost: "I came in second," he said, "and my opponent came in next to last!"

Tearing a page from the politician's manual, we can coax, tease, and tame words to make them work for us, and so build up a strategic vocabulary through which we can say anything, anywhere, anytime and still win friends and influence people—those closest to us most of all!

The ancient Greeks set three basic guidelines for effective communication: *ethos, pathos,* and *logos.*

Ethos is the distinguishing attitude; it is a reflection of our character and sets the criteria of where we are coming from. It is objective rather than emotional. It is the root of the word "ethics," which is the tone of our moral philosophy.

Pathos is the emotional—the empathy, sympathy, understanding, and compassion which, although it woos the person one is trying to reach, is also sensitive to their perspective. In simple terms, when love is felt the message is heard.

Logos is the word in which the ethos and the pathos are expressed. It is the root of the word "logic" and is the reasoning and controlling influence behind what we say.

When we incorporate these three guidelines into our thought patterns and our dialogue, we establish an effective, strategic base of communication.

Fortunately, at times of frustration when we need them the most, God sends us life-changing communicators to teach us.

When my daughter reached that critical age of slouching posture and a spotty skin and I got sick and tired of screaming, "Stand up straight!" and "Scrub your face!" I decided that I would let someone else do the screaming for me. I marched her off to charm school.

Most of the charm in the charm school was in the

charm of the director who *never* screamed, "Stand up straight!" or "Scrub your face!"

Instead, she looked into our daughter's eyes and said, "Nile green—just like Queen Nefertiti of Egypt! Do you know that in the Middle East women speak with their eyes?"

Then she took her hands, looked carefully at them, measured the length of the fingers against the palm, and like an impressario discovering an unusual and rare talent, exclaimed with genuine delight, "Beautiful hands, and such long artistic fingers—you are a very creative person! Now let me see . . . shoulders here, yes—that's just right. You will make a dramatic model."

She did not say "good." She did not say "beautiful" or "successful," she said "dramatic." She aerated her statement and allowed for lots of flexibility, imagination, and conjecture by the use of a very strategic word. She eliminated the negative (she never mentioned the spots), she accentuated the positive, and . . . our daughter's shoulders never slouched again and she scrubbed her face until the skin nearly came off!

Not only our daughter went to charm school—I found that I was going to charm school in a spin-off course as I sat in the parent's waiting area week after fascinating week, a mesmerized observer.

A gala presentation was the highlight of each season. As terrified little girls with heads drooped down and eyes glued to the floor walked the runway at their first crack at a public appearance, they were announced by the director over the P/A system. "Elizabeth has the most beautiful smile—show us, Elizabeth!" The eyes and head came tilting up and the smile gleamed wide to relax a tense and frightened face.

Chubby, gawky girls were generally given the prettiest of the dresses to model to boost their morale, and as they waddled under the spotlights, emphasized in the commentary were the lace, ruffles, ribbons, and color that "Susie (or Patsy or Debbie) brings alive!"

There were no chubby, gawky, waddling little girls in the vocabulary of that director. Nor were there any skinny, stringy, clumsy little girls. All we heard was "Tracey who has been so helpful to me this week," "Janet with the naturally curly hair," or "Karen . . . how she loves animals!"

Gone were the "uglies." Girls were described as "sparkling," and they suddenly became "sparkling" (sparkling ugly, but sparkling nevertheless!). The prettiness of the pretty little girls was not emphasized; it would have been too contrasting. Instead their best feature or the gentleness of their nature became the focal point.

There were times I resented that director. I wondered if she ever blew up, lost her cool, yelled and screamed and carried on, or felt like cracking heads together!

She did get angry. Sometimes she set her lips in a firm straight line, brought the class to a screeching halt, and waited in articulate silence until, one by one, the students got the message and toed the line. (How many times since, when the rowdies became impossible to cope with, have I pulled the car over to the side of the road and waited; not one inch forward until the hubbub was subdued.)

When she spoke, students listened. If they didn't she would just lower her voice so they would have to be quiet and attentive in order to hear, and she would be very sure that she said something that they were anxious to hear—such as just when the television camera was to arrive so that they could see themselves on the screen (always a highlight).

To her each little person was a special opportunity for a mysterious and magical transformation and the motivation that stretched them toward their very best potential was positive, strategic words.

That lady was *ethos, pathos,* and *logos* the like of which is seldom found! She could have sold snow to the Eskimos, negotiated a permanent peace with any nation on earth, and through her carefully chosen words made friends of enemies and devotees of friends.

She had a respect for the universal gift of individualism, an empathy and understanding of the sensitivity of human nature, so easily bruised, and she had developed a strategic vocabulary of encouragement that always built up rather than tore down. The best part was she meant every word she said and her love was real.

She changed my attitude, my vocabulary, and thereby changed my life. I sift through my words. I strain them like a prospector searching out the gold and dumping all the dross.

The common denominator of a strategic vocabulary is the word *courtesy.*

The nicest words said rudely become the rudest words.

Among best-loved royalty in England is Elizabeth,

the Queen Mum. When she reigned and her daughter (the present Queen Elizabeth) was just a little girl, they were shopping in the famous Harrods Department Store in London. A flurry of clerks followed them around, ready to be of service and most anxious to please. After one frustrating encounter with a fumbling clerk, the young princess was irritated and impatient—she spoke up rudely. Immediately she received a reprimand from her mother.

"But . . . I'm the princess," said little Elizabeth with a pout.

"Royalty," replied the Queen Mum, "is no excuse for bad manners!"

Courtesy can take the most difficult of words, the most controversial, angry, and unpleasant words, and translate them into discretionary form. It does not necessarily diminish their meaning or the content of their message or compromise intent; it merely takes away the sting.

Take the word "unfortunate." Rude, gauche, stupid, irritating, asinine, obnoxious people were described by my mother as having a "most unfortunate manner." Somehow it suggested that they were victims of their own rudeness rather than perpetrators, and it stirred pity and compassion rather than resentment and anger. It was the courteous difference between "He's a blithering idiot!" and "He has a most unfortunate manner!" (He was, of course, a blithering idiot.)

"Awkward" was another favorite. When I behaved badly, instead of yelling that I was an insolent, spoiled brat, she would grasp me firmly by the hand, put steel in her stare, and snap, "Stop being awkward!" It covered many sins. And "awkward situations" covered many situations.

Bad behavior was always "inappropriate." I could be rolling on the floor in a temper tantrum, but it was never "terrible," "awful," "gross," or "horrid"— just plain "inappropriate."

One of the most volatile of words in a strategic vocabulary is one of the smallest—it is the word "*but.*"

"*But*" can be a joy-sapper, a heart-in-mouth gagger, or a lift-me-upper.

As a lift-me-upper:

It is difficult, *but* you can do it.
You've missed the plane, *but* there is another in half an hour.

As a heart-in-mouth gagger:

There's no need for you to worry Mom, *but* . . .
I know I'm calling after midnight, *but* . . .
The car is OK, *but* . . .

As a joy-sapper:

I love your dress, *but* haven't you put on weight?
You did well, *but* you should have done better.
I love you, *but* there are times I don't like what you do.

The last statement is widely used and generally accepted, but it is a joy-sapper nevertheless.

"I love you" is unconditional or it is not love. Love has no ifs or buts. Unless embellished by a positive, "I love you" requires the finality of a period or the joy is sapped out of it. When linked to a negative, this is especially so.

"But" is a word of such high intensity that whenever it is used, what is said after it tends to wash out what has been said before it. (Unless of course the statement is, "I am giving you five thousand dollars, *but* be careful how you spend it!)

Strategically, by a simple reversal a joy-sapper can be turned into a lift-me-upper: "There are times I don't like what you do, *but* I love you!"

Words are the romance of language. They court it like lovers jostling for attention!

Scathing sarcasm is devastating and has no place in any vocabulary, strategic or otherwise. Humor, on the other hand, is essential.

Fun words often crack up tight walls of tension and provide the way out of a hostile confrontation.

Our daughter wanted to change her given name. She went through years of hating it and we went through years of trying to make her like it. It was a sticky issue. For us, it hurt because she was rejecting what we had spent many delightful months searching out and choosing. For her it was the anguish of whether to hurt us that way or to free herself from an almost moment-by-moment articulated irritation. The guilt and tension on both sides kept building to the point where the mutual frustration became abrasive hostility. One day my husband had had enough.

"Call yourself Phoebe Ambidextrous Tilligas or anything you like," he said. "A rose by any other name will smell as sweet and we will never stop loving you!"

She changed her name, and Phoebe Ambidextrous Tilligas has become a family joke. Now, just to tease, we sometimes call her P.A.T. for short!

In everything we do and say, we can do it kindly in the kindest way. Why hurt when we can heal? Why tear down when we can build up? With *courtesy* as the common denominator and *kindness* as the ground rule, the words of our mouths and the meditations of our hearts become pleasing not only in the sight of the Lord, but also to the person to whom they are addressed.

Words can make us or break us.

"Was it something I said?" You bet it was!

The Courage to Be Authentic

When we see ourselves as others see us, that is self-concept. When we see ourselves as God sees us, that is self-authenticity!

It was a time for the color purple and a special fragrance. Jacaranda trees hung heavy with blossom and shed fragile purple bells to lay a soft-hued carpet underfoot. Ladies of the Nile clustered in stately clumps, flaunting starbursts of as many as thirty slender lavender flowers from a single stalk. Beds of iris, pansies, and the almost hidden violet splashed royal colors along the sidewalks on the city streets.

Wisteria was in bloom, creeping through fences, trellised over arbors, and here and there smothering out a front porch. The ultimate display was a dazzling canopy of color hanging shades of delicate purple over the entirety of one full acre—all from the single vine that got our small town into the records of Ripley's "Believe It or Not."

It was a time of "flower children," with gypsy skirts and flimsey see-through blouses, butterfly-seat jeans with mushrooms stitched defiantly through the crotch. Bare feet walked the canyon paths, winding serpentine through the hills just behind our home.

In sharp contrast to the purple fragrance that hovered over the city like some anointed blessing, the canyon air hung sullen with marijuana and the stench of fermenting garbage, scattered helter-skelter through the wasteland of drug-filled, spaced-out, fermenting lives.

From that ferment came a howling, an arrogant baying that thumbed its nose at the passerby, "Back off and butt out! I am what I am, and I don't give a damn for that what I am!"

In the midst of the howling, like the calm in the eye of a storm, a quiet voice replied, "I do. I gave the entirety of all that I am for that what you are. I will never back off. I will never butt out."

There is no defense for the love of God.

She fell into our living room one night, hungry and lost. Her eyes were wild, dilated into two deep, dark tunnels leading to oblivion. They were haunting, desperate eyes on a young and frightened face. She had lost her job (junkies don't last long in jobs), been tossed out of her home ("How much more can we let her steal?"), and isolated by society. Tumbling down into the squalor of drugs and self-abuse and stirred raw in a subculture at the bottom of a pit of pits, she tried time and time again to claw her way up, only to be pushed back down by the banality of her own inadequacy and a self-contempt that screeched at her, "You are not even a zero. You are a *minus* on the scale of life, a worthless, hopeless nothing!"

We are confluent beings, inherently connected—we build each other up, or we tear each other down.

She saw herself reflected mirror-vision in the eyes of those around her as an exercise in futility—torn down, useless and utterly despised. Sitting on the floor in our living room, a crumpled, disheveled heap, she pounded her head against the smooth velour of a worn-out couch as though she would, if she could, knock herself completely out. The only prayer that she could pray was, "God, if you love me, kill me, because I don't have the guts to do it myself!"

God did not kill her. Instead he pursued her with a flaming love to melt the ice around her frozen soul.

God is God of the second chance. He is God of the fall-and-I-will-pick-you-up-again third chance. He is God of the seventy-times-seven I-love-you-too-much-to-ever-let-you-go chance!

He is hope of the hopeless.

That night a crumpled, fractured girl whispered, "Even me, Lord?"

"Oh child of my heart of hearts," His still small voice replied, "I am waiting here for you."

That night a bruised and wounded girl gathered up the splinters of her shattered self and one by one she dropped them at a pair of feet nailed to a cross.

She let go of guilt and took instead . . . forgiveness.

She let go of fear and took instead . . . faith.

She let go of weakness and took instead . . . strength.

She let go of hate and took instead . . . love.

She let go of the past and took instead . . . a hand to guide her through the present.

She let go of everything that she was and took instead . . . everything that Christ could be within her.

Love reached down, and God came in and filled the void whose shape is God.

All the worthlessness of who she saw she was in the eyes of those around her became instead all the priceless, irreplacable worth of who she saw she was in the eyes of God—she made that vital change of focus from temporal to eternal.

When we see ourselves as others see us, that is self-concept. When we see ourselves as God sees us, that is self-authenticity!

God sees us with the eyes of love.

It is a love of affirmation. Father Brennan Manning, a priest who has a ministry of healing through affirmation, tells us that we need to remind ourselves daily of God's intense love:

God loves me. He loves me beyond my worthiness or unworthiness; beyond my fidelity or infidelity. He loves me without caution, regret, boundaries, limits, or breaking points. He loves me no matter what I've done with my life. . . . God cannot stop loving me!

God loves me whether I am in a state of grace or disgrace; whether I live up to the lofty moral expectation of the gospel or I don't. He loves me with a love that keeps no score of wrong. . . . A love that loves with such disarming simplicity, such unaccustomed tenderness and such infectious joy that it wrings from even the most calloused heart, inexpressible bursts of joy, gratitude and wonder!

It is a love that loves us just the way we are, but it is a love that loves us too much to leave us the way we are. It gently moves us from being . . . into becoming . . . all that we can be.

DEVELOPING A SENSE OF SELF

The essence of being is a recognizable identity, a sense of purpose, and an ultimate destiny.

Our recognizable identity is our *sense of self*.

We have to live with ourselves, so it is vitally important that we know who we are living with.

When I was just a little girl, prone to bad behavior, my mother would look me squarely in the eye and say, "Come along now, snap out of it and be yourself!"

I was never quite sure just who the self was that she was telling me to be, but I was very sure that the self that she was telling me *not* to be, a mean, nasty self or a whining, grousing, pouting self, was not my real self. And if my real self was not that, well . . . it must be quite the opposite—a nice and decent self.

This was the strategy she used for building into the self-image of a naughty child qualities to reach for in developing a self worth living with.

Through the years she kept it up. She would make excuses for me: "Well, Fay is not herself today." Or more directly, "Let's talk about it when you are more yourself."

This was her way of saying that a perverse, cranky, or unreasonable state of being was a state not worth being in and that I should expect better things from myself . . . reach for a self beyond myself.

Our *sense of self* is the synthesis from which we view the world around us and all the people in it. It is the perception on which we build all that we are and all that we can be.

We have three selves within us—the self we were, the self we are, and the self we would like to be.

When Eleanor Roosevelt graduated from finishing school in England, her headmistress sent her off with the challenge, "Be all that you can be!"

But for most of us, the crux of the matter is "What is all that I can be when I don't even know who I am?"

We stand befuddled, like Cathy in the comic strip: "I work. I eat. I sleep. I stay in touch with family and friends. These four things take me full-time. There's a world of news, art, science, and music going on every day that I miss. A whole universe of ideas and information goes right by me because it takes me full-time just to get through the four main things I have to do. I'm a four-channel receiver in a 198-channel world."

We have 198 channels (more or less) crowding in on us. They fragment our time and prattle a thousand voices, throwing up images and impressions against which we juggle the concept of our many roles and selves, until we become confused and consumed by all that is exterior. We lose our grip on that vital cortex around which our lives revolve—our inner *sense of self*.

There is a tremulous state of self that Anne Morrow Lindberg describes in her book *Gift from the Sea* as *Zerrissenheit*—the German word that means "torn-to-pieces-hood."

"If one is out of touch with oneself," she says, "then one cannot touch others. . . . Only when one is connected to one's own core is one connected to others."

She found that her core, her inner spring, was nourished through solitude, taking specific times in her life to isolate herself spiritually from those around her to rediscover her *sense of self*.

It is from the wellsprings of our soul that we find our *sense of self*.

We are not the creation of a divine caprice; we are the carefully planned reflection of a divine Providence who loves us with an unconditional, desperate love, and who hyphenates our individual identities to his own divine nature.

Compacted into the functional vehicle of our human body are the attributes of God: our mind, the intelligence with which we think; our heart, the seat of our emotions with which we feel and respond; and our will, the root of our character with which we choose and decide. These make up our soul, into which God has breathed the human spirit that yearns to be filled with the divine. It is that void, the emptiness within that is never filled until it is filled with God.

The life-changing transposition that moves us out from under self-doubt and extends to us the grace of divine possibility happens when we empty self of self, so that we may be filled with the divine self of God.

Self-surrender to a loving God is not self-abasement; it is self-fulfillment . . . self liberated from its own constraints and weaknesses and authenticated for the specific purpose for which it was created. It is an emancipation that frees us to be all that God would have us to be.

Handing one's self over to God is the magnification of the One who dwells within us. Only then can we sing out with Mary, "My soul doth magnify the Lord, and my spirit hath rejoiced in God my Savior!"

Our *sense of self* becomes directly related to our sense of God.

Self-surrender is an act of surrender of the will. Whatever or whoever controls our will, controls us.

I was a self-willed child, or so my mother used to tell me. She told me that all her life, usually accompanied by a melancholy sigh, and it seems that my willfulness grew in consistancy with my age, so that the child in me when I was forty-five was no less aggravating to the parent in her than when I was only five.

We locked horns, she and I. The arrogance of my will pitted against the authority of hers in that rub of flint on flint that kept the sparks flying. We fought the good fight, and it was a "good" fight that developed in my character a stubborn streak, a determination to scrutinize, analyze, make my own decisions, and then hold on ... regardless of the consequences.

Neither of us was a milquetoast; it was one strong will thrashing it out with another strong will in that awkward perversity that balances between love and hate, friend and foe.

Yes, I *was* a willful child! I found out at a very early age that what makes us or breaks us, pulls us up or drags us down is the determination of our will.

A crucial test came when I was only ten. A group of boys in the compound (cluster of houses) where we lived had found a snake and killed it. They were running to and fro, jabbing that poor dead snake into girls' faces just to hear them squeal, throwing it around their frightened necks, or putting it down their backs, all of which if done to me would have been nothing short of instant death—I am deathly afraid of snakes.

I had two options: I could die or fake no fear of snakes. I chose to fake it. Before they came running at me, I started walking slowly toward them, "Please, let me hold the snake," I shouted. "I would love to see it!"

They jabbed it in my face, "Yah, yah, here it is!"

I did not flinch or hesitate, although I am sure I must have blanched. With my heart racing and my tongue swallowed halfway down my throat, I took that snake in both my hands and held it for an endless moment—cold scales, clammy against my sweaty palms. I can feel it even now and I want to shriek and let go!

I am still afraid of snakes, but now I know that through the exercise of my will I can handle snakes. And if I can will to handle snakes, then I can will to handle almost anything!

God can mold a strong will (yes, even a stubborn, tenacious will) when it is turned towards him. . . . but God has no use for self-will, that petulant arrogance that says, "Me, in my own way."

First Church of the Nazarene in Pasadena dominates the landscape with a silver-domed roof from which a stained glass turret beacons hope and help for miles around. Fifty-two yellow rose bushes highlight eight red rose bushes in a special garden that is a memorial to the tenacity of will, endurance, and sacrifice of the fifty-two American hostages held captive by Iran and those who gave their lives in the unsuccessful rescue attempt.

Gary Lee was one of the hostages. His father was pastor of that church during those fateful and faith-filled 444 days. Each morning Earl Lee raised the American flag, putting his prayers into every star and stripe. He lowered it each night. It became tattered and shredded by the force of thunder showers, Santa Ana winds, and the blazing, scorching heat of the California sun, but still it went up and came down with the steadfast regularity of a heart and hand that would not give up.

From the very beginning of the ordeal, Earl and Hazel Lee determined by an act of their joint will that the one thing they would not think or say was "What if?" What if Gary was being tortured? . . . What if he had been killed? . . . What if he never did come back? . . .

They placed Gary (and the other hostages) in the only arms capable of holding him and sustaining him through those long traumatic days—in the arms of a loving Lord. They wrapped him in their prayers, believed in the strength behind that flag, and held on to the supremacy of the overruling will and power of a sovereign God.

When Gary was released and came to Pasadena, all whoopee broke loose! Yellow ribbons festooned the trees, yellow balloons hung huge golden puffs up in the sky, and one family's faith joined the faith of a nation in services of thanksgiving. And all of that is significant to Earl and Hazel Lee and to the parishioners and people of that church, but behind that significance is the vital core of a commitment that took them through the anguish of those days and will take them through the anguish of any other days or any other trying circumstances of their individual and joint lives.

If you visit there you will catch it in the regular singing of a simple song of faith. The words and music were written by one of their parishioners, Lynn Edward Keesecker.

I'll say "Yes, Lord, yes,
   to Your Will and to Your way"
I'll say "Yes, Lord, yes,
   I will trust You and obey;
When Your Spirit speaks to me
   with my whole heart I'll agree,
And my answer will be yes, Lord, YES!"

The surrender of our will to the will of God is a commitment that does not say, "What if?" but raises its flag of faith and puts its prayers into every tatter and shred.

I am still a self-willed child. Moment by moment I bend that will to the sovereignity of the will of God. I sing along with Earl and Hazel Lee, "To Your Will and to Your Way . . . I will trust You and obey . . . yes, Lord, YES!"

DEVELOPING A SENSE OF PURPOSE

"Would you tell me, please, which way I ought to go from here?" said Alice to the Cat in *Alice in Wonderland*.

"That depends a good deal on where you want to get to," said the Cat.

"I don't much care," said Alice.

"Then it doesn't matter which way you go," said the Cat.

If we don't much care, it doesn't matter which way we go, but, like Alice, we might end up having tea with the Mad Hatter!

Our *sense of purpose* is set by where we are coming from and where we intend to go.

God in Christ became as we are, so that we in Christ can become as he is, possessed of a unique dignity given only to the human being, that makes us the reflection of the presence of God among us and participants in his Divine purpose.

The Christ-filled life does not abdicate our originality, personality, or natural God-given ability and merge us into one huge blob of sanctimonious conformity—that would be deathly dull! Instead, it takes what we are and holds up Christ as a mirror-image. We reach for all that we can be when we reach to be more and more like Christ.

In setting life directives and goals experts tell us that we should project a distant view and then work backward. When we are lighting the candles on our eightieth birthday cake, what do we want to say we have accomplished? Then we back up. Where would we like to be twenty years from now? Ten years from now? Five? Three? One? It's a countdown to what we should be doing this year to reach what we would like to be doing next year.

A *sense of purpose* is the driving force within our lives that pulls out from us all that we can be.

Whatever our long- or short-range goals, we are programmed for purpose and productivity, whether it's digging up a weed, decorating a cake, running a marathon, writing a book, making a fortune on the stock exchange, having a baby, or learning how to play the piano ("I've always wanted to," one woman confessed, "and now at last I'm doing it!" She was 65! And from a young mother having just achieved the goal of having a baby, "My life goal has suddenly become sleep! Will I ever be able to?").

From my early teens I wanted to write. It became for me a *sense of purpose.*

"I cannot write a book," I told myself, but then I

realized that I could share my thoughts and experiences, that I could write a paragraph; so I set a goal to sometime in my life write a book.

I started practicing by writing paragraphs, floating paragraphs, sometimes totally unrelated to each other. On the days when I could not even write a paragraph, I thought, "but I can write a sentence!" So I wrote a sentence—one scrawny sentence to cheer me up and cheer me on, something like, "Hello. I'm the first subtle sentence of your new paradoxical paragraph!"

Then I found myself talking to that cockeyed sentence, telling it what I wanted to say in hackneyed phrases and words that jiggled around pell-mell all over the page. Some words I plucked from a list of challenging words that I keep with a goal of using them, words like "preposterous," "boondoggle," and "periwig" (Ha! There, you see I've used three of them and so achieved a short-term goal. Those three words have been on my list for two years waiting to be used! Now if I could only find a place for "umbrage" and "zooecium" . . .).

The paragraphs started following each other like tin soldiers marching in a line, and before I knew it, the thought I was groping for started to jell and I had a chapter, then another and another (then I would read them over, scratch them up, and toss some out to start again . . . and again . . . and endless times again) until finally, voilá—I had a book!

Each of us has been carefully and peculiarly made (some more peculiarly than others), each endowed with specific abilities and talents. We are all one-of-a-kind designer originals (you alone are you!). We can all do something and do it well.

This is the diversity that unites us all as human beings. It is the enchanting and curious individualism of our multifaceted personalities projected through a variety of abilities that keeps us from boring each other to death and God from yawning.

In developing our work goals job guidance counselors tell us that the ultimate would be to find something we enjoy doing, learn how to do it well, and then find someone who will pay us for doing it!

Years ago I jotted down a quote in my notebook that has served me well all my life: "Practical people are those who know how to get what they want. Philosophers are those who know what they ought to want. Ideal people are those who know how to get what they ought to want!"

Success is not necessarily setting the world on fire— success is heart contentment.

Spiritually, we process our life goals and directives through the will of God. This sends the desires of our heart running downstream to merge in the current of God's plan for our lives . . . which makes for a very exciting *sense of purpose.*

When I am heading off in the wrong direction, I trust God to set up the roadblocks and turn me around. I also trust him to clear the way ahead when I am moving in his perfect will.

The vital fact is that until we get in motion, he does not have the opportunity to direct us. We won't go anywhere if we don't get in the car, turn on the ignition, give it some gas, and . . . then ask God to take the wheel.

Once on the road and moving, God will direct us. We yield at the yield signs, pause at the stop signs, detour around the roadblocks, and sometimes find we have to back up and turn completely around to head off in a different direction!

At other times we read the road map wrong, but the old saying is still true—"Better to fail in trying to succeed, than to succeed in failing to try!"

I learned a lot from a young high-school band member due to march in the New Year's Day Rose Parade in Pasadena. His group had practiced all year for this big event. Their uniforms were stunning and they had made the trip to California half way across the country, paid for by self-sacrifice and a variety of fund raisers. Now the weather looked inclement.

"What will you do if it rains?" he was asked.

"Get wet and keep right on marching!" he replied.

When the clouds of disappointment hover overhead, and it threatens to rain on our parade, we get wet and keep right on marching in step with the will of God.

As our children became teenagers, we gave them each a plaque to hang in their rooms. It is a familiar quote and it is the foundation of our *sense of self* and our *sense of purpose.* "What you are is God's gift to you. What you become is your gift to God."

In all our becoming, Jesus sets the pace. "The Son can do nothing of himself . . . I can of mine own self do nothing." (Jn. 5:19, 30) Jesus was totally subservient to the will of God.

We are the glove into which the hand of God will fit.

The miracle is that in each of our lives, for the plan and purpose of that life, it is a perfect fit.

We lay all the finite fragility of all that we are and the availability of all that we are on the altar of a commitment that simply says, "Use me, O Lord . . . use even me."

He does.

He doesn't have to, but he does . . . and that is the magnificence of his grace.

Our hands rest passively by the side of our body waiting with the reflex of an instant response the command from our head. As the glove containing the hand of God, we are to be passively available, yet constantly alert to his commands.

In our over-anxious efforts to fulfill God's purpose in our lives, and to please him, we have the tendency to dance the fingers of our glove constantly in front of his eyes peskily chanting, "What will I do next . . . what will I do next?"

Our dog Scooter is a pesky dog. She is a pretty dog, with long black silky hair and a wistful expression. She is a devoted dog, so much so that she follows me around from room to room and becomes a shadow self that nearly drives me mad. She tries to please— almost too hard.

She loves to play ball, but instead of waiting for me to actually throw the ball, she is overanxious and takes off in the direction she thinks I am going to throw, to get a headstart. Then she sniffs around pitifully, wondering where the ball went when all along I still have it in my hand.

Stupid? No, just trying to please (my husband says "stupid," but then he has a grudge—she threw up once all over his car). If Scooter kept her eye on the ball held firmly in my hand, she would know exactly when and where it was thrown.

When she does get the ball, she brings it back but frequently won't let go, refusing to listen to my command to drop it, until I have to pry it out of her mouth with great discomfort to her jaw.

I like to get a headstart on God. I am anxious to please.

"You have a plan, Lord? I am your person." I rush out in the direction that I think he is going to throw. I develop strategies and scurry about trying to nose things out, and then I wonder, like Scooter looking for the ball that is not there, why the plan does not work. God pulls me up short, "Fay, look. My plan is still here in my hand!"

And then there are the many times I have refused to let go.

"Thanks," says God. "You've carried the ball and done your part. Now for heaven's sake let go!"

I have learned that it is not much fun to get my jaw pried open by the hand of God. There is pain involved.

One hand does not take its instructions from the other hand. My left hand cannot make my right hand do a thing. This is not to say that we do not work together as many hands. Hands need other hands . . . try tying a shoelace or threading a needle with only one hand. Many hands do make light work, but individually in our personal walk with the Lord we take our instructions and directions from the head and the head of the body is Jesus Christ.

We encourage each other, we exhort each other, we pray for and help each other, but God forgive us when we try to manipulate each other.

God gave each bird its *own* wings with which to fly.

I am an avid birdwatcher, and the garden is quite full of them. Each variety flies with a different style. The most astonishing flight comes from the smallest bird, the little hummingbird. It is capable of flying backward as well as forward, straight up and down, and hovering in place motionless save for the blur of its whirring wings—a most versatile flight.

I have a friend like that. I send her hummingbird pins and cards and think of her as God's dainty yet most versatile and capable little person.

Another friend I call a "golden song bird." She has a lovely voice and her life is a beautiful flight of encouragement and love. Then there are the chickadees, winsome, perky friends who cheer my heart and flutter more than fly.

Some of us are made with strong powerful wings, capable of soaring high and long or catching a breeze so that we can go a great distance with hardly flapping our wings at all. Others of us dart about on short hops, from bush to bush and tree to tree. Each of us has wings designed exactly right for us to be all that we are meant to be and to take us where we need to go.

Jesus singled out the sparrow, the small and commonplace bird found almost everywhere. "I see the sparrow fall . . . " he said. Somehow I think he sees us all as sparrows!

However strong or weak our wings, it is when we use them to be the bird he designed us to be and fly toward him that we reach for our ultimate destiny— to nest securely in the heart of God.

Running Around in Spiritual Circles

The epicenter of the spiritual circle is the redemptive love of Jesus Christ. It has a ripple effect to reach out and encircle us, whoever we are, wherever we are, and to draw us into the heart of God.

Whatever circles we happen to run in, one thing is sure, sooner or later they'll show up under our eyes!

Taking the inside track and leaping over the hurdles of the great Denominational Divide, running around in spiritual circles activates our adrenalin, accelerates our heart rate, and pumps fresh air into tired theological blood.

Running in circles makes for a very well rounded person.

The more we meet, greet, eat, and retreat, the more well rounded we become, especially around the waistline. Taking as a scriptural base, "Thou shalt not live by bread alone ... " we add baked potatoes with sour cream, chicken cacciatore, and apple pie à la mode. This accounts for so many pudgy people in the pulpit and in the pew and is part of the expanding girth of the spiritual circle.

The spiritual circle rotates on the axis of the word *evangel*. It comes from the Greek root meaning bearer of glad tidings (as at Christmas) or messenger of good news (as at Easter).

The epicenter of the spiritual circle is the redemptive love of Jesus Christ. It has a ripple effect to reach out and encircle us, whoever we are, wherever we are, and to draw us into the heart of God.

"How will people believe if they don't hear?" asks the apostle Paul. "And how will they hear if nobody tells?"

The show and tell of the good news of the love of Jesus Christ is what keeps us running around. This means that the spiritual circle revolves concentric with the witness of the speakers' circle.

I entered the speakers' circle at a very early age. As I yakity-yakked my way through adolescence, demerits emblazoned themselves on my report cards, often accompanied by the terse comment, "Fay has a tendency to talk too much."

My parents called it being "full of the blarney," a throwback to the Irish side of our family. My husband calls it "never being able to get a word in edgewise." And my children call it "please get off our backs!"

When I first believed in my heart that Jesus is Lord and took up the call to confess him with my mouth, I surrendered to him my gift of gab. This catapulted me into the spiritual speakers' circle, where I soon found out that most of the running around there is done on the knees.

Rule One of the speakers' circle is pray. Rule Two is prepare, and Rule Three is don't take a laxative the night before!

Effective communication is sincere conviction given with grace from one heart and received by another.

The great American essayist Ralph Waldo Emerson describes the eloquent person as one who is not necessarily an eloquent speaker, but one who is inwardly drunk with a certain belief. Fidelity to that belief and the desire to share it brings an impassioned eloquence that moves and motivates the human heart.

Mother Teresa is a perfect example of this. After she had won the Nobel Peace Prize she was interviewed on a Canadian television station where she shared the program with a geneticist who had won a Nobel Prize in science. In describing the talk show, Malcolm Muggeridge (author of the book on Mother Teresa *Something Beautiful for God*) said that the geneticist made the point that all our destinies are built into our genes and there is nothing we can do to alter this. "All pure nonsense and humbug!" comments Muggeridge.

Mother Teresa just sat there with her head bowed praying. Toward the end of the program the interviewer asked, "Mother Teresa, have you nothing to say?" She looked up and said, "Yes. I believe in *love* and *compassion*," and then she went back to her prayers.

The witness of her faith was caught in the simplicity of two words—more eloquent than volumes! By enfolding herself in prayer and then stating as simply as she could those things she passionately believes in, Mother Teresa is, in the words of Muggeridge, "the most formidable witness to the Christian faith that you can imagine."

She spent the entirety of the talk show (we may surmise at least half an hour) in prayer and no more than ten seconds in articulation—a staggering ratio equal to four days in prayer for every half hour of public speaking!

In spiritual circles, no matter how lucid, how credible, how carefully researched and presented, no matter how polished or persuasive, unless our words of witness are anointed by the Holy Spirit they are lifeless, hollow words. Likewise, unless the hearts of the audience have been anointed to receive the words given out, they fall on hardened stony ground and will not take root. This is what makes the prayer teams preceding an evangelist around the world so essentially and vitally important.

Conversely, the anointed words of Scripture coming from many an unanointed speaker have reached out to change countless lives. This is the magnificence of the grace of God, a grace that chooses to use not only the flawed vessel, but even the flaws in the flawed vessel.

God promises that "as the rain and the snow come down from the heavens and do not return without watering the earth, making it yield and giving growth to provide seed for the sower and bread for the eating, so the word that goes from my mouth does not return to me empty without carrying out my will and succeeding in what it was sent to do" (Isa. 55:10–11, *Jerusalem Bible*).

But prayer alone is not enough.

The integration of prayer, preparation, and practice is the power behind the podium and the speaker's platform.

A reporter once asked the famous playwright George Bernard Shaw how he developed his marvelous gift for oratory. Shaw replied that he learned to speak as people learn to skate, "by doggedly making a fool of myself until I got used to it!"

When the Lord calls us to publicly share the witness of all that he has done within our lives, it is a noble opportunity.

Speaking is merely thinking out loud, so we had better think before we speak! It's too easy to fall into the trap of not knowing what we are going to say before we say it, not knowing what we are saying while we are saying it, and by failing to come to a comprehensive point, leaving the hearer blank and confused by not knowing what we have said once we have said it.

Wise is the speaker who prepares a message outline, point by vital point, preens it with illustrations to which the audience will relate, and then thinks about it and visualizes it until the message becomes not only a living part of the speaker, but the speaker becomes a living part of the message.

Then comes a flexibility of spirit, an openness to be swayed by the anointing of the moment. This makes our witness given over and over again at many different times and places under varied occasions and circumstances always new and fresh, which is surprising, sometimes to the speaker most of all!

In spiritual circles, mere rhetoric is not enough.

Mother Teresa does not only practice what she preaches, she preaches what she practices! Her living out her message comes before her speaking out her message; indeed she does not have to speak at all. *Love* and *compassion* are the very breath of her being and with them she has run a circle of healing care and comfort around a hurting world.

The witness of how we live our lives is the undergirding witness of our words.

Whatever track we happen to run on, in spiritual circles we are all encouraged to *run*. It is part of running the good race. Not that we get the runaround, although sometimes we do.

Of the many tracks within the spiritual circle, the academic circle is one popular spin-off. The Bible calls it studying to show ourselves approved. The world calls it going around on the carousel of learning prior to turning the wheel of fortune.

Regardless of what it is called, to parents it is the circle that puts many more circles underneath their eyes as it circulates their kids in ever widening circles and their money in never ending circles!

The first hurdle on the academic track is the aptitude test—as in, "Your aptitude tests show that you will do well in a profession where your father holds a position of influence."

The final hurdle is commencement—as in, "Most everything you've learned will be of no use to you at all, except that when you graduate you will be able to tell when someone is talking rot . . . and that is the purpose of education!" (Commencement speaker to Oxford University graduates.)

No one runs in academic circles. Academic circles move very slowly. They are usually a stop-and-go experience with more stops than goes, especially when it comes to term papers, final exams (traumatically known as "in the pit stops") and such seemingly trivial things as financial aid and the final payment due before graduation.

Seeing as my encounter with compound fractions and split infinitives left me with an acute allergy to academia, I try to stay off the beaten track of the academic circle.

The closest I have come was a run-in with Harvard. One summer our sixteen-year-old son took a tour of historical America with his high-school class. They spent a day at Harvard and as a souvenir of his visit to that prestigious campus, he brought back a red sweatshirt with *Veritas Harvard* stenciled in an arc across its chest. When I threw it in the wash, the color ran and dyed all his underwear bright pink (which put him in the loser's circle when it came to showers in the P.E. locker room!)

This proves that despite any rumors going around that Harvard might be radical red, when it comes down to hanging out their dirty laundry, Harvard is only slightly pink. Whatever red it might have embedded in its *Veritas* will all eventually come out in the wash!

Evangels who go around in academic circles generally prefer to do so in a seminary where everyone majors in Greek.

The seminary track runs in two directions. The conservative track is canted to the right and runs clockwise, ticking off the countdown to the millennium. Liberals, on the other hand, tend to lean to the left and run in much wider circles, which makes for a lot more exercise.

In order to keep a theological equilibrium, it is a good idea to reverse tracks once in a while and run in somebody else's direction.

This is called balancing a perspective. The only

caution is that there might be a tendency to spiral right out of the circle and end up instead on a tangent that runs through sticky, controversial places. These cause a lot of runners to get stuck in a rut and spin their spiritual wheels.

When this happens, both conservative and liberal runners get cranky and exhausted and end up muttering aggravating things to each other, such as "in the generic sense" and "inerrency." But if they had stayed on their own track, they would continue to wear comfortable smiles and twiddle their complacent theological thumbs.

Unlike the stop-and-go experience of purely academic circles, in spiritual circles we are told to pull out all the stops and "press on toward the mark for the prize of the high calling of God in Christ Jesus" (Phil. 3:14).

In every race there are winners, losers, and also-rans. Most of us are also-rans, but the best part of running in the good race is that it promises that the first shall be last and the last first, which, loosely translated, means that we don't know exactly where someone like Oral Roberts will come in, but you and I are assured of a place up front in the Kingdom of God.

This goes to show how much God loves even those of us who drag our feet.

One of the reasons that we drag our feet is because we are carrying too many weights.

Paul tells us to lay them aside, and strip off anything that slows us down or holds us back, especially bad habits that tend to wrap themselves tightly around our feet and trip us up. He exhorts us to run with patience the particular race that God has set before us, always keeping our eyes on Jesus who is our coach.

Weights, like calories, creep up on us and need to be thrown off daily.

Each morning I go through a weight reduction program. Physically I jump on the scales and groan, "That settles that—celery and carrot sticks for me today!" And emotionally I analyze what weights I am carrying and why. Many of these need dealing with before they can be thrown off.

In American Indian culture one healing process in dealing with the afflicted is to encourage them to dig a hole in the ground, lie down on their stomachs, and speak out loud into the hole all their negative thoughts as well as their fears, frustrations, discouragements, and anger. Then they cover the hole over with dirt and "bury" the stressful emotions that are a hindrance to a state of well-being.

A good idea.

However, in throwing off our emotional weights, we need to take caution that those that need dealing with are first resolved before they are buried alive, where they will surely take root and grow again.

Appropriate negative emotions generally have good reason behind them; they are friends of the human condition. Dr. Willard Gaylin, an ethicist at the Hastings Center in New York, tells us that guilt, for example, is one of these. In his article *In Defense of the Dignity of Being Human*, he explains: "Guilt is a uniquely human emotion that demands expiation for wrongdoing. It implies that we have internalized a set of noble standards by which we judge ourselves and that if we have done wrong we punish ourselves."

Animals do not feel guilt; they feel fear. If a dog

digs up a plant in the garden as a continually re-
peated offense and it knows that it is going to get a
whack as punishment, it will probably cringe in fear,
not guilt. A dog cannot say to God, "Forgive me for
not behaving like the type of a dog you would like me
to be!" Guilt is a gift of human conscience.

Gaylin makes reference to what he calls one "outrageous" self-help book in which there is a chapter
describing guilt and anxiety as useless emotions.
"Since anxiety is the principal emotion serving individual survival, by eliminating these," he says, "the
author has eliminated two of the foundation struts
on which survival is built."

Thank God for the guilt that motivates us to right
a wrong, make an apology, confess a sin, or ask
forgiveness.

Healthy guilt is our friend; it is unhealthy guilt
inappropriately carried that is the weight we need to
throw off. Examples are the guilt of a sin long since
confessed that God has forgiven and forgotten but
that we dig up again and again to brood over and
carry like an albatross around our neck, or the guilt
of regret about a circumstance over which we really
had no control.

It is interesting to note that the Chinese word for
"stress" or "crisis" is composed of two characters, of
yang and yin: *danger* and *opportunity*. We can take
the *danger* signals of our negative emotions and turn
them into *opportunities* that work for us.

Simmering anger is frequently the dangerous hedge
we cultivate to shield ourselves from emotional pain.
Some people are, as one psychologist put it, "excep-
tionally even tempered—always angry!"

Instead of letting anger gnaw away at our emotional gut, we can turn it into the opportunity that pulls us toward the catharsis of a long overdue confrontation.

Loneliness, instead of squeezing the joy out of our soul, can become the motivation to become involved in giving ourselves to serve others, such as visiting the sick and elderly or writing to service personnel overseas, many of whom never get a letter.

Depression, that bleak grey web that entangles us and holds us immobile, is often a biological danger signal to get a check-up and verify that our hormones are jumping and our juices flowing. It can become the opportunity to reach out and say "I understand" to others who may be going through the same dark mood.

Frustration turned from being a bitter enemy in my life into becoming one of my best friends.

Frustration is the godfather of innovation!

I was caught in the vise of not enough time and not enough done. I prayed constantly that God would multiply my time and it seemed that instead he multiplied my commitments.

"Slow me down, Lord," I cried. Instead he replied, "I will teach you stamina and endurance, and you will learn how to run faster!"

The pace of my race quickened and pressures crowded in on me to the point where I felt as though I was being crushed into a corner where I would stifle from lack of space and ventilation. Yet there seemed no way of escape.

"How do you cope?" I asked a busy executive. We were having dinner together as I listened to a staggering list of involvements that ran him in circles around the world to the extent that he seemed to spend more time in the air than on the ground! Almost daily he faced desperate crises of disaster, hunger, flood, drought, and endless human trauma and anguish. These pulled against him in conflict with the ever present priority of his family commitments. Yet he seemed so calm, so "in control."

"I have learned," he said, "to deal with only one thing at a time. I keep a mental file cabinet with my involvements and commitments carefully categorized in separate drawers. When I need to think about something and deal with it, I take it out, handle it, and then I put it back and shut the mental drawer on it until the next time it needs attention."

I have learned his art of opening and shutting mental drawers and switching emotional gears. No more dithering. No more wasted thought.

Instead of continuing to be frustrated by the stress of the daily mess that seems to clutter my life, I am learning time management.

For example, instead of operating on a hit-and-miss basis (with more misses than hits and frequent ten-dollar late charges) I take one day a week (Monday) to pay our bills, answer my mail, return phone calls (unless urgent), stock the larder, run errands and generally clear the decks . . . a whirlwind of activity! These used to have me puttering around daily in a dither, huffing and puffing, bucking confusion and resentment.

Frustration turned from being the weight dragging on my skirts like a tugging, whining child into becoming the motivation that continues to teach me the discipline of rapid-fire organization.

God was right. I am developing stamina and endurance and running faster—spiritual sprinting! The best part is, I am enjoying the race.

The weights that pull us down are not the appropriate negatives that we can and should handle, but the inappropriate negatives that slay us emotionally—other people's choices that hurt us as well as hurt them, brooding resentment (dead weights that if we don't bury them, they will surely bury us), a consistent cantankerous, negative attitude that always fears the worst, instead of looking for the best.

These will not only slow us down, but unless they are thrown off they will bring us to a full and complete stop.

What we cannot do anything about, we can lay at the feet of a Savior who has promised to carry our weights for us. He as our burden bearer will pick them up and do for us what we are unable to do for ourselves, or for someone else.

The second lap of running the good race is fighting the good fight.

Fortunately Paul clarifies this by telling us that the fight is "not against people made of flesh and blood, but against persons without bodies—the evil rulers of the unseen world, those mighty satanic beings and great evil princes of darkness who rule this world, and against huge numbers of wicked spirits in the spirit world" (Eph. 6:12, *Living Bible*).

On the one hand, this is a great relief, as it eliminates our need to look at all our neighbors and go, "eenie, meenie, minie, mo," as to who might be on which side of the fight and has us concentrate on loving them instead. But on the other hand, it is disconcerting to fight against persons without bodies—we could easily bump into them without being able to say, "Excuse me," which might make them very angry and vindictive.

Being vulnerable to attack by things we can see is bad enough, but being attacked by things we can't really sets our faith aflutter. Indeed, this is one of the most severe tests of our spiritual mettle.

> From ghoulies and ghosties,
> Long-leggitie Beasties
> And things that go bump in the night . . .
> May the good Lord deliver us!

We fight the good fight with the sword of the Spirit, which is the word of God.

It comes sheathed in the American Standard Version, the Living Bible version, the New International Version, plus many other versions, all of which are the contemporary no-frills counterpart of that grand old traditional version, the highly ornamented and richly embellished King James Version.

Whatever the sheath, the sword of the spirit is not meant to be sheathed, it is meant to be drawn out and held forever *en garde*.

One of the most deadly swords ever in existence is that of the Samurai. It has a blade that is razor sharp and is strong enough to lop off a head with one forceful blow.

The Samurai were among the most feared warriors in the world—the mere mention of their name would send tremors through the heart of the enemy. The power behind their combat was not only courage, strength, and strategy; they knew how to use their sword to its best advantage. But many other warriors were as well equipped and trained. What made the Samurai warrior such a dreaded enemy was the fact that under the code of the Samurai, warriors considered themselves already dead, so they had no fear of death. This gave them a fierce abandonment in battle and a ferocious vigor in their charge against the enemy.

We fight the good fight with the same abandon and vigor. The name of Christ and the razor-sharp sword of the world of God is the code under which we fight—it sends terror through the hearts of our enemy.

Fortunately in our combat the only heads we are to lop off are those of the extraterrestrial beings that tend to not only go bump in the middle of the night, but that bump into us at all hours of the day as well—the principalities and powers, rulers of darkness not flesh and blood, and spiritual wickedness in high places (hopefully very, very fly-away high places!). These are the mischief makers who stir evil in our lives.

In his preface to The Screwtape Letters, C. S. Lewis says, "There are two equal and opposite errors into which our race can fall about the devils. One is to disbelieve their existence. The other is to believe and to feel an excessive and unhealthy interest in them."

Prior to and during World War II Helmut Thielicke, a Lutheran professor of theology at the University of Hamburg, ministered throughout Germany. He observed the rise of Hitler and the Nazi movement and was a witness to what he said were very real demonic powers at work. Hundreds of thousands of good people became corrupted and controlled by what he calls mysterious abysmal powers leading them where they had no intention of going. In his sermon "Deliver Us from Evil," he says "Behind all the dangers in our lives, and behind the dark menaces that overshadow it, there is a dark mysterious, spellbinding figure at work. Behind the temptations stand *the* tempter, behind the lie stands *the* liar . . . "

He describes Satan as a master of disguises and says that one of his tactics is to hide behind seemingly positive values and ideals. Demonic forces of evil do not identify themselves as evil, they infiltrate us with delusions and deceptions that appear to be good.

They masquerade as angels of light, bringing what they call "new insights," which are in reality twisted false doctrines that have just enough scriptural truth in them to make them intellectually palatable.

Thielicke gives the illustration of the hordes of people, most of whom had been brought up under Christian influence, some even baptized and confirmed, cheering themselves hoarse in auditoriums over the German faith-movement and other of Hitler's pagan ideologies. If the devil had to carry a passport, Helmut Thielicke tells us, under the descriptive heading on it of his special characteristics there would have to be listed "none." He assumes whatever characteristics that suit his purposes of deception.

Evil influences in our lives appeal to our intellect, our aesthetic as well as our base appetites, our emotional vulnerabilities and offer "something interesting," "something pleasurable," or something that will give us "a glorious thrill and the chance to live to the full!" They woo us with anything and everything that will lead us further and further away from Christ and erode the solid bedrock of scriptural truth.

Jesus was not exempt from this attack. When he was tempted by the devil in the wilderness, he showed us the way to complete victory. His three rebuttals were his skilled use of the word of God: "*It is written*, Man shall not live by bread alone, but by every word that proceedeth out of the mouth of God. . . . *It is written*, Thou shalt not tempt the Lord thy God. . . . *It is written*, Thou shalt worship the Lord thy God, and him only shalt thou serve" (Matt. 4:4–10).

We deflect, parry, and pierce the evil influences in our lives with the sharp edge of the Scriptures.

When we are consumed by unnatural or unholy fears, we thrust out with a Scripture such as "Greater is he who is within me than he who is within the world" (1 John 4:4, personalized).

When temptations to sin, whether in thought, word, or deed, fill our imagination with lascivious thoughts, we can renew our minds with "casting down imaginations and every high thing that exalts itself against the knowledge of God, and bringing into captivity every thought to the obedience of Christ" (2 Cor. 10:5). And then, we deliberately set our minds to think about what Paul describes in Phillipians 4:8 as "whatsoever things are true, . . . honest, . . . just, . . . pure, . . . lovely, . . . virtuous, . . . and good."

The mind is the battleground where we fight the good fight—the victor wins control over the heart and soul.

The good news is that when we submit ourselves to the overruling control of Christ in our lives and resist the Devil, he will flee (James 4:7)! Like the legend of Dracula—when the cross was held up to the vampire, he turned in fear to cover his eyes with his cape and shrank quickly back into the shadows!

Christ has already fought and won the good fight. We participate in his victory when we use as our arsenal a bouyant consistent prayer life coupled with a diligent study of the word of God.

The word of God separates truth from error, it confronts, convicts, and convinces, and it encourages and uplifts.

It is the sword of the Spirit that so pierces a heart with the love of God that in being wounded it is totally healed, in losing all that it has it wins all that it can never lose, and in dying it becomes eternally alive!

Come Ride The Rainbow &
Brighten Up Your Life!

The rainbow is "the smile of God." It meets us where we're at and leads us on with strength for today and hope for tomorrow. It is the light of heaven shining through the prism of our tears to scatter brightness on our path.

Some days color me blue. The sun may be shining, the bees buzzing, the flowers blooming, but who cares. Turn the world slowly, I want to get off!

"I'm not alone," I whimper into my coffee. "Thousands all over the country have staggered to their feet this morning and faced the same grim fact—there's a pit at the end of the rainbow, and I'm in it."

The vital question is not so much how I fell in—whether I was pushed, tripped, toppled, trapped, or even whether I crawled in on my own volition, like a wounded animal looking for a dark and lonely place in which to nurse a crippling hurt—but rather, once I'm in, I'm in, and . . . how do I get out?

"If our dreams don't come true, we can be thankful that neither do our nightmares." (Dr. Laurence J. Peter). When Atlas shrugs, and Homer nods, God frequently winks. To capture the twinkle in his eye, we dig in our spiritual spurs and harness up to the rainbow of his promise.

The rainbow is "the smile of God." It meets us where we're at and leads us on with strength for today and hope for tomorrow. It is the light of heaven shining through the prism of our te[...] brightness on our path.

The rainbow may begin in a pit, [...] aboard it lifts us up through the m[...] faith, to the pot of gold which is [...] who cares.

In reaching for God's promises [...] the seven basic characteristics of his infallible divinity: his *justice* and *holiness*, which means that he cannot deceive us; his *grace* and *goodness*, which means he cannot forget us or shove us aside—God is committed to love us; his *truth*, which means God cannot lie, or change—he remains steadfast in the promise of his word and we can depend on it; and finally, his *providence* and *power*, which means he has made provision to care for us—he superintends our lives and he has the ultimate power that enables him to accomplish.

These are the toeholds that give confidence to our hope and boost us up from the depths, so we are able to sing with the psalmist, "O my soul, don't be discouraged. Don't be upset. Expect God to act. For I know that I shall again have plenty of reason to praise Him for all that He will do. He is my help! He is my God!" (Ps. 42:5–6, paraphrased).

At those excruciating times when my heart ices up in my chest and the pit I have fallen into is so deep it seems to have no bottom, when thoughts jumble together to numb my mind beyond coherence and tears become the only language my heart can speak, I remember . . .

She is a small woman, thin almost to the point of being scrawny, with sharp birdlike features and eyes constantly searching for a vision beyond the ordinary. In her convent school days she took a lifetime vow: to hold her soul free in the face of changes of fortune. Up until she was ninety years old she plunged daily into the ice-cold waters of Cape Cod for a vigorous swim and went for a three-mile walk.

Motion was for her an act of courage. "I have to keep moving, walking, pulling away at things, praying to myself while I move," she said, "and making up my mind that I am not going to be defeated by tragedy." This was the self-discipline that she integrated into every aspect of her life. She toned herself—body, mind, emotions, soul, and spirit—to a responsive harmony that synchronizes two essential elements of an indomitable faith: courage and determination.

She has needed them.

Her husband spent the last eight years of his life incapacitated, unable to speak or move without help and she was constantly by his side. One daughter is retarded, and after years of struggling to keep her at home, she went through the heartache of having her institutionalized. She did not doubt God's goodness. She said, "If anything it strengthened my belief and sheltered my spirit from despair. . . . The more I thought, the clearer it became to me that God in his infinite wisdom did have a reason, though it was hidden from me, and that in time, in some way, it would be unfolded to me."

Another daughter was killed in a plane crash, and her eldest son was blown up in World War II. The assassin's bullet cut down two sons in the prime of their manhood, to wring not only the grief out of her own heart but to forever stain with tears the memory of a nation.

Day by day, hardly skipping a beat, Rose Kennedy, grand matriarch of the famous clan, put on her modest chapel veil and went to prayer. She placed the confidence of her hope and strength in that sevenfold justice, holiness, grace, goodness, truth, providence, and power of a God who does indeed hold her soul forever free. He has kept her twinkling, riding high on the rainbow of a promise that says, "Come. Bring everything to me."

In an interview with Cleveland Armory for *Parade Magazine*, she shared her hope for the ongoing generations of her family. She hoped they would "have the strength to bear the inevitable difficulties and disappointments and griefs of life, bear them with dignity and without self-pity, knowing that tragedies befall everyone and that although one may seem singled out for special sorrows, worse things have happened many times to others in the world, and *it is not the tears, but determination that makes pain bearable.*"

"Birds sing after a storm," she says, "why shouldn't we?"

If there are two words that should be said in the same breath and said regularly to ventilate our hope, that should be flamed together, branded as a signature of our faith, they are the words *faith* and *courage*. It takes courage to believe, and in order to have that courage, we must believe!

In the bottomless pit courage is sometimes a roar of fear as it clutches its own tail, like the cowardly lion in *The Wizard of Oz,* and screws its eyes shut tight to pace a determined step, stammering through chattering teeth, "I do, I do, I do believe. I do, I do, I do . . . "

Courage is knowing the limits of our endurance yet taking the hand of faith to stretch beyond them, and the staying power of that faith is the resolve of a solid, persistent determination that says it's always too soon to give up!

"Never give up!" thundered Winston Churchill in the midst of the heat of battle, "don't ever give up. Never, ever give up."

Toward the end of his life, he was asked by a schoolboy, "Sir, what is the greatest thing that you have ever done?"

Churchill could have opened up a portfolio of dazzling accomplishments. He could have pointed to the blood, sweat, and tears of the agony of war. He could have orated his famous, "never have so many owed so much to so few . . . " But his answer braces us with the chill of its stark reality.

"The greatest thing that I have ever done," he said, "is to survive, because to survive is to begin again!"

We tend to remember the glory, the accolade of his moment in history. We tend to forget the years he was jeered in the House of Commons, and he survived to begin again. He suffered times when he was ridiculed and booed and heartache when he was rejected at the polls, and he determined with a solid resolve never ever to give up, but to begin again, and again, and again.

Determination is the stamina that separates the winners and losers in life. It is the buoyancy that is the difference between swimming with our heads one inch above the water or sinking with our heads one inch beneath the water.

Determination strokes our survivor instincts and is the momentum that lifts us up out of the pit of depression and defeat and up onto the rainbow of promise and hope.

At those exhausting times when my determination lags, when my head tells me all the right things, but my heart screams pain that runs sand through my veins to weigh me down, when I am left holding together the ragged edges of a wounded spirit, and I want to let go and give up, when courage becomes merely a rhetoric beyond my grasp, I remember . . .

Ruthie is tall and walks with her head held high and a straight back—a model's gait made graceful through years of carefully measured movement. Her eyes know sadness, yet in their dark reflected light there is a spark of fire. Beneath her bottom lip, canted slightly to the side, a tiny mole teases smiles—a wink of God twinkling from her lovely face. She is a woman beautiful and beloved.

It was the witching hour, the middle of the night when darkness runs deep, dreams splash vivid, and consciousness stands still, when fearful shadows cloud the banks of memory and we wake, struggling for breath and floating in a sea of sweat—confused as to what was and what is and feeling the foreboding of what might yet be.

I woke with Ruthie running through the limbo of my night; her eyes were full of pain and her face was bathed in tears.

Does God still speak in dreams, or do the demon dancers whirl, like dervishes, to intersect subconscious thought? Which angels keep the watchtower of our soul to shake us out of reverie and call us to our kne...

"... ?" I whispered into nothing... a frightening urgency, I wen...

He... later and therein lies the telli... nary *faith, courage,* and deter...

Ru... it to go. They had been just t... ld think of a thousand thing...

"Ple... agging, "come with us. You ca... y and it's much more fun when y...

It wa... ey did things together, but riding... ng up the dust around the eight-m... of El Mirage and up and down what the kids called the "whoops-de-doos" of the crusty terrain of the California desert rattled their bones and stretched tendons they did not even know they had.

"Just be glad they still want us with them," said Ruthie as she packed the big orange van with fresh linen and a few extra pillows to cushion the bumpy ride home. "Time will come soon enough when they don't."

That settled it—they would go.

The Dyches were a root'in toot'in family. They celebrated each other with fierce loyalty. Whatever they did, they did with gusto and gave it their best shot.

They laughed easy and cried easy, and maybe that's what kept their yard full of kids and their kitchen bustling with activity.

They lived on the wings of a prayer and a song, riding high on the rainbow of promise.

The prayer was usually Roy, reading out of the big family Bible. Then they all clasped hands around the dinner table to give thanks, first of all for each and every person there and then for the blessings of the day.

The song more often than not was Ruthie banging away on the piano leading a fest of old familiar hymns: "The Old Rugged Cross," "His Name Is Wonderful," or "There's a Sweet, Sweet Spirit in This Place." The kids would strum on guitars and thump on the drums, and others who happened along tapped their feet, picked up on the beat, and joined in, while Hans, the family collie, dragged his tail between his legs and found a friendly bush to crawl under—preferably as far away as possible from the deafening din.

At fifteen J. R. (Roy, Jr.) was six feet tall and still growing. Warren was eighteen. He was what Roy Dyche called a "heart-brother," that is, not blood-related family, but more family to the Dyches than many who were blood related. A husky six foot four, he had arms and shoulders that rippled with muscles that flexed ramrod steel. He could load the Yamaha and Suzuki onto the van with ease and maneuver a bike with all the finesse of an expert rider. Dave Hall was a tag-along buddy. He was also eighteen and was the one who introduced dirt bikes into the Dyche family.

It was a hot night, so still that the occasional burst

of laughter from campsights across the lake bed carried miles, piercing shrill on the desert air.

"It'll be a scorcher tomorrow, that's fur sure," said Roy.

They were setting up camp on the low rise of a hill, tucked back in an isolated spot off the main drag.

"Look," said J. R., pointing to the full moon. "God turned the light on, up in the sky! Let's take one quick ride before we turn in."

Moonlight was magic that night. It's radiance pushed back the stars and danced shadows behind every bush. It threw an eerie silver glow over the rocks and dunes—enticing! It was a night for wonder, for adventure, a night for anything but bed.

Ruthie dragged out the helmets and started digging for the rest of the protective pads and biker gear.

"Forget it, Mom," said J. R. "We're just taking a short, safe spin—no fancy stuff I promise." He pulled on a T-shirt. Warren was ahead of him, gunning his bike, his bare chest tanned bronze from the California sun, glistening beads of sweat.

"You all go. I'll stay here and watch our stuff," said Dave. He was stretched out on his sleeping bag, one hand pulling on the ear of Hans, who nuzzled him, poking for a game.

Ruthie and Roy climbed into the dune buggy and followed close behind the boys so they could throw out a beam from their headlights to cut a swath of light ahead. They criss-crossed down the center of the lake bed, a pair of moon warriors revving their engines and flashing silver chrome to dominate the night.

"Glad we came!" smiled Ruthie as she reached over

and gave her husband's arm a squeeze. On the turn back, heading towards their spot on the hill Roy lost sight of the boys.

"Drat it!" he grumbled. "They should have known to stick close to us."

"Maybe they've taken a roundabout route and will come up from the other side of the campsight," said Ruthie shunting aside a quiver of fear that trembled in her throat.

As the dune buggy started to climb the riser, out of the corner of his eye Roy caught the sparkling red glint of a small reflector. He spun the buggy around and threw up the high beam. The reflector was clipped to a barbed wire fence. It had the extra long barbs and heavier twist of the type used to contain cattle. Its three strands were strung unusually close together.

"Danged peculiar spacing," growled Roy. "Mean looking, and danged dangerous place for a barbed wire fence!" He turned off the engine, leaving on the high beam to illuminate the fence, and he listened for the sound of the bikes that should be coming up the hill.

Silence. Articulate, terrifying silence.

"Must have gone a different route," he muttered. He felt a knot in his belly like a vise, twisting and tightening a sickening grip. He dimmed the lights and stepped on the accelerator, "Let's get back."

When J. R. came to he was lying on his back looking directly into the moon. Searing pain was burning up his chest and in his head sharp daggers were exploding through his ears. He lifted his hand and saw blood trickling through his fingers.

"I'm dying," he thought. "I must be dying . . . "

Then he heard the cry, faint as though coming from a long distance away. "Roy . . . Roy . . . help me. I'm hurt bad."

"Warren!" Where was he?

Staggering toward him no more than twenty feet away was a grotesque monster with glazed eyes bulging out of an ashen face. His chest was slashed, dangling bright red ribbons, and blood dripped rivulets from a ring of chewed-up flesh around his neck.

Warren was first one through the barbed wire fence.

He and J. R. had made the turn well ahead of the dune buggy and picked up speed for the climb up the hill. By the time Ruthie and Roy saw the reflector, the boys had burst through the fence and were lying in the darkness some two hundred feet away just out of range of the angle of the beam of light.

The first wire caught Warren in a whiplash that coiled around his neck, biting and tearing with deadly barbs. The second and third wires, strung at chest and waist level, clawed grisley diagonal stripes across his body, mauling him like some carnivorous jungle beast. He fell to his knees, looking at the horror of his bloodied chest and moaned strange gurgling sounds.

J. R. had caught the backlash of broken wire. It flayed his chest and arms. Skid burns blistered huge strawberry patches down his back.

"We're both going to die," he thought, "right here, bleeding to death, sponged up by the desert sand."

Sobs wracked his body. Then he heard his father's voice coming at him through the years, "You can always do whatever you have to do. God will give you the strength."

Determination reached for faith.

"We gotta make it," he muttered. "God, please help us make it!"

"Warren," he shouted, "get up!"

He crawled over and shook him. Warren was staring at his chest mesmerized by his own bloody wounds, swaying and groaning as if in a trance. J. R. crouched and, flinging one of Warren's massive arms around his shoulders, he heaved . . .

"Shut your eyes and don't look . . . just lean on me and walk!"

Warren shut his eyes and staggered to his feet. He thrust the bulk of his weight on the younger boy. Reeling with pain, together they walked, stumbling toward the nearest light.

The light came from the pup tent of Dr. Tom Henderson. He had gone to the desert to write and he cussed the *vroom* of the engines when he heard the bikes.

"Blasted intrusion on the environment," he thought.

Now, lying on his sleeping bag dictating into a recording machine he saw another intrusion—two interlocked figures coming right at him, like specters in the night.

Holding up his kerosene lantern he gasped as he saw the bloody slashes. His medical instincts bristled an immediate response . . . stop the bleeding and hit the hospital—fast!

He had only the very basics in a first-aid kit with him. Wadding gauze into the largest hole in Warren's neck, so deep that it exposed the jugular vein, he tried to staunch the flow of blood. Then he hoisted the boys, literally by the seat of their pants, and flung them into the back of his truck.

J. R. pointed weakly to the light on the hillside. "That one . . . there."

Dave Hall was the first to see the headlights in the distance, coming up the hill much too fast. Hans had been howling for several minutes and Ruthie clutched Roy, "Honey, maybe Hans knows something. I'm scared!"

Dave jumped on his bike and raced to meet the truck.

"I'm a doctor," yelled Tom from the truck. "I've got the boys. Run up ahead and get your people ready to take them to the hospital; they're in bad shape."

Roy kicked open the back doors of the van and started throwing everything out but the pillows that Ruthie had laid end on end, fresh and clean—an astonishing eight of them.

"My God," she prayed, "please . . . let everything be all right." But everything was far from being all right.

"Listen carefully," said the doctor as they made the transfer from truck to van. "Take a deep breath— you *must* handle this."

"Jesus, sweet Jesus, please help us," sobbed Ruthie. When she saw the mangled boys, she felt her insides falling apart. "I've got to be strong," she determined, "Lord, help me listen carefully and not let the boys see my fright."

Kneeling in the center of the van she had a boy on either side of her. One hand, using its fingers as a clamp, was holding Warren's neck wound shut. The other held J. R.'s chest together and she had to give him a shake every once in a while to keep him from losing consciousness. J. R. was going into shock.

Tom leaned over the driver's seat and pointed Roy down the road. "The closest hospital is Victorville. When you hit the main road, turn left and you'll start seeing the signs. I've done all I can. I'll stay here with Dave and watch your things. God go with you."

Every bump on the desert road brought a scream of pain from Warren. "Stop, stop," he'd yell. "I can't stand it!" Then he would jerk upright, rigid, and Ruthie would lose her grip on his neck so the blood oozed out while she struggled to "talk him down." The fresh clean pillows were drenched with blood.

"Pray for me," Warren moaned.

The tears were rolling down Ruthie's cheeks, her eyes were full of pain. She could not bear to look at what her hands were holding; she felt squeamish and giddy and was afraid that she would faint. She shut her eyes.

"Lord, you said that when we need you, we can call on you no matter where we are or what our circumstances are. You said that you would help us and be our strength in time of trouble. We take that promise now. O Lord, we're in big trouble. Be with us. Take the wheel of this van and put Roy on the right road to the hospital. I can't hold on much longer. Please hold together the edges of these wounds for me and stop the bleeding. Please, please, come to us!"

A strange hush fell over the van, and suddenly it was filled with another presence—someone had come in!

Ruthie's hand, numb from clamping her fingers tightly to close the gap in Warren's neck, felt another hand holding it. The numbness left and the feeling came back. Her back, tense and cramping from her awkward position, relaxed.

J. R.'s eyes were full of tears. He was awake, alert, and looking at her—he had felt it too!

"Roy," Ruthie whispered, awed by the sound of her own voice, calm and in control, "do you sense someone else in the van with us?"

"Yes." Then, his voice choked with emotion, Roy began to sing softly, "There's a sweet, sweet Spirit in this place, there's a sweet, sweet Spirit in this place . . . " Ruthie joined in, her beautiful contralto blending a perfect harmony, " . . . and I know that it's the Spirit of the Lord!"

With each line of the familiar chorus the pitch rose in confidence and strength until they were smiling and singing at the top of their voices. J. R.'s lips were mouthing the words. The family was okay. They were once again living on the wings of a prayer and a song, riding high on a promise that said, "I am with you—always!"

They kept singing, not after the storm like the birds, but in the middle of the storm, piercing through the dark clouds with the brightness of their faith to call from the heart of God—a rainbow. Only Warren was silent; he had passed out.

They had been driving for over an hour and there was still no sign of the hospital. Roy pulled into an all-night market on the corner of an intersection. There was only one other person in the parking lot, a man getting out of his car.

"This is an emergency," yelled Roy. "We have two kids in the van hurt bad. Can you point me to the hospital?"

"More than that," the man yelled as he got back into his car. "I'm a paramedic. I've just got off work. I drive one of the ambulances. Follow me, it's right up the hill!"

"Thank you, God," Ruthie whispered. "The only person we see turns out to be a paramedic . . . I know you have taken control of this van."

J. R. suffered a minor concussion and had a hundred and fifty stitches across his chest and arms. Warren had four hundred stitches in his neck alone; over the rest of his torso there were just too many to count. He seemed to be in surgery forever. For once, being without a protective helmet providentially saved his life; the extra weight would have snapped his neck. Again, providentially, the barbed wire had been weakened, crudely welded together in two places; had it not been, it would have decapitated him.

Almost a year to the day the boys went back to the fence. They knew they had to do it. "We can't let it get the better of us," they said. They rode their bikes up to the break in the three strands that had been repaired, again crudely welded together at neck, chest, and waist level. "Mean looking . . . " They faced it, square on. This time they were wearing their helmets and protective biker gear. They took one long minute of confrontation, then with a holler and a whoop they spun their bikes around and zoomed to churn the dust of El Mirage.

When I am flayed within my soul, and hurts gape

wounds I cannot even bear to see, when I fall, swaying and groaning, mesmerized by fear, and feel that I would die, sponged up in a desert place, God puts his arms underneath my life and heaves me up.

"Shut your eyes and don't look . . . just lean on me, and walk!"

When my determination lags and pain like sand runs through my veins to weigh me down, Ruthie runs across the limbo of my night. Her eyes know sadness and beneath her bottom lip, canted slightly to the side, a tiny mole still teases smiles—the wink of God twinkling from her lovely face. There is a sweet, sweet Spirit in that face, and now I know . . . it is the Spirit of the Lord!

I ride the van with her, praying all the way and holding on.

I've learned to sing a simple song of faith, not after the storm like the birds, but in the middle of the storm, piercing through the dark clouds, to call from the heart of God the promise of his rainbow.

Living on the Edge of Tomorrow

When our hearts are crouched up in a corner and our minds blinded with delusion, we pray "Come, come, Lord, with your shining light!" and because he is the Lord of hope, he comes.

They say that before he sat down to write anything difficult Martin Luther placed a flower across his desk. It served to soften his somewhat tempestuous temperament and keep his perspective in balance, so that no matter how heavy a storm was brewing deep within his soul, he should focus always on the beauty and goodness of God.

With this in mind, and setting about to write something difficult, I have placed a flower across my desk—a rose, creamy yellow, to bring the sunshine in.

I picked it fresh this morning—an out-of-season rose, blooming in the chill of a winter's day. It tells my heart that joy, like the rose, can pierce through the cold, cold places frozen in our memories and bloom when least expected, that rain, torrential blinding rain that lashes up against us and buffets us about, is the same rain that falls deep into the earth to nourish the beautiful blossom of the rose. It tells my wounded spirit that for all the beauty of its bloom, until the rose is most severely torn apart and crushed, we cannot extract from it the essence of its fragrance.

The garden is soft with morning light and a row of pigeons sit along the chainlink fence taking a shower in the spray of water tossed up like diamond drops by the sprinkler head. They lift one wing coquettishly, holding it poised like a feathered fan spread open, and then the other, up and down, up and down, in a fluttering wave that makes me laugh. Isn't it droll that birds wash underneath their arms!

When the sprinkler is turned off the sparrows will come to the birdbath just beneath the window where I write and perch in a semicircle around its rim. They twitter up a merry chatter as one after another takes its turn to jump in and splash about—like little girls gathered at a public pool to play a game and gaggle over giggles.

A half-moon bridge is set among the ferns with a small marker. The marker seemed appropriate. It is an antique iron scroll salvaged from an old estate. "The kiss of the sun for pardon, the song of the birds for mirth, one is nearer God's heart in a garden than anywhere else on earth!"

The garden is so tranquil now.

It was not always so.

It is two years ago, almost to the day.

He came by early in the evening to pay his rent. He was dependable, on time. A handsome man, in his prime. A good tenant. The lawn was mowed, leaves raked, and garden kept—the sort of thing that makes for a good tenant.

We had rented him the small cottage just six months before. It seemed exactly right, close to his job, a good job, good for him and good for us.

"And how's it going, Jim?" I asked with that casual nonchalance that says nothing, means nothing, and expects nothing in reply.

"Fine, fine . . . " he said, giving me a darting look and a quick smile as he wrote out the check.

Now, on thinking back, was there a fleeting quiver in that smile?

It was Henry Thoreau who said that the mass of us lead lives of quiet desperation. Does desperation come cloaked in smiles that flash bright teeth against the smoothness of olive skin?

He turned and waved a small gesture of goodbye, and I watched him walk slowly down the driveway to his car. He did not slump. Why, I was to wonder later, did he not slump? He should have slumped. He sauntered, swinging his hips to ripple the clean-cut line of a worsted suit.

"We must have him up for dinner," I said to the family gathered around the table. "It's not easy, you know, to batch it, all alone."

I said that every month. Hollow words, they fell out of my mouth like bits of lead. I never did invite him in, not even for a short sit and brief exchange of pleasantries.

Why, I ask myself, a thousand times why? What if I had? What *could* I have said? What *would* I have said? What *should* I have said?

The call came at three in the morning. The body is at its lowest ebb in the early morning hours—a suspended state. The blood runs slow and reflexes are sluggish.

"Fay, come quick! Jim has blown the house apart and set himself on fire!"

With what must have been a great effort he had

used a heavy wrench to uncap an old gas outlet just inside the front door. As the gas spewed up, collecting at the ceiling and making its way through the vents up into the small attic, he had gone back to the kitchen and lit all the burners on the gas stove—turned them up high.

Then he had taken seven hundred aspirin, mashed them into a watery paste to more easily force them down.

He lay atop his bed and waited . . .

What thoughts chewed on his soul as he lay there listening to the hiss of rushing gas?

Had he awakened in the early hours with a lonely scream swelling up inside him? Was it a terrifying dream that sat upon his chest and leered? Or the prospect of another dull day locked into yet another in the endless routine of a wound-up life that puts us through our paces until suddenly, unwound, we stop? Was there no one to talk to, no one to understand, no one to say, "I care"?

Turgenev, the great Russian novelist said that he would give all his fame and fortune for someone who really cared whether or not he came home at night.

Did he pray? I think he prayed.

Or had he snapped—beyond thinking . . . beyond feeling . . . beyond anything but the abrasive pain of loneliness?

When the gas worked its way down to reach the fire burning on the stove, the explosion blew out the entire front of the little house. It fell into the garden, splintering glass and shooting pieces of debris like flaming arrows to set the shrubs on fire. The cottage was cleanly sliced down the front like the cut-away of a doll house, with open access to every room.

It takes a particular combination of oxygen and gas to cause it to explode. The explosion sent great balls of fire popping into the air, a spectacle of whirring colored light against the darkness of the early morning hours. Jim, his clothes and hair on fire, staggered as though blown onto the center stage of a blazing holocaust.

There he stood, a human torch, arms raised up in supplication.

The firemen reached and pulled him down.

It is suffering that makes dying an act of love and mercy.

Brutally burned, Jim died that night. He teetered over the edge of the anguish of one lonely day pushing against another; the edge of tomorrow moved just beyond his grasp.

Looking through the charred and blistered shell, all that was left of the little house, over the neat, trim garden now strewn about with rubble, I saw a squat rose bush out of the corner of my eye. It sent up yellow buds of hope rising audaciously from the desolation.

We have rebuilt the broken house. It's better and stronger now, with lots of light and a bay garden window.

The yellow rose I placed across my desk I picked from that selfsame bush that bloomed then, its buds rising up from despair. It has grown taller now and throws up armloads of flowers, still audaciously blooming out of season to bring the scent of springtime into a chilly winter's day.

This little house is the studio where I write. My typewriter is set almost to the very spot where Jim cried out that night. He lives in every word I write.

Though torn apart and crushed, he sends a special fragrance wafting through the rivers of my memory. And I ask myself a thousand times what *could* I have said? What *would* I have said? What *should* I have said?

Suddenly I know—too late for him, but time enough for someone else . . .

"Come on in and sit a while, and talk."

When the hurts of today have drained our endurance and we are crushed and broken by despair, when we feel ourselves frozen in an emotional paralysis that numbs our senses so that nothing works, our arms and legs hang limp and even our eyes slump back into our heads, we grope for the edge of tomorrow. It's promise of a new beginning is only a day away and it's resource is hope.

When we think that we have nothing left, we need to remember we still have hope.

The poet Emily Dickinson wrote:

> Hope is the thing with feathers,
> That perches in the soul,
> And sings the tune without the words,
> And never stops at all."

Hope is the gift of anticipation that keeps our hearts alive. It is the very antonym of despair.

Despair brings a self-estrangement that digs a pit deep within the innermost parts of our being and then fills itself with fear and trepidation. It backs us up into a corner, powerless to rise to our own self-defense, so that we enter that dark night of the soul when (as someone wrote to tell me) "even our prayers seem to fall like dead birds out of the sky, splat at our feet instead of rising upward."

Locked into lassitudes of despair, we find ourselves becoming party to our own disintegration, and hope slithers about, slippery in our grasp.

One of the chief causes of despair is an aching loneliness—the need to reach and touch and to be reached and touched, to hold and to be held.

We are social beings. In his book *Alone with the Alone*, Father George Maloney says:

The most pathetic and heart-rending suffering in human lives comes precisely in the context of human love. That which God meant to be an incarnation of his trinitarian self-giving as two human beings give to each other the gift of themselves in an *I-thou* relationship moving towards a *we* community so often becomes a living hell of self-estrangement or lonely isolation.

"Do you know what it is like to be lonely all your life long?" one man asked. "I do. Do you know what it is like to be always on the outside looking in and no matter what you do, not being able to get in? I do."

A little boy named Richard said he was lonely too. From an emergency shelter for abused and neglected children, he wrote:

Lonely is waking up and having no one to say good
    morning to.
Lonely is not having a father there to play ball with
    when you were little.
Lonely is sitting in your room on Christmas day
    wishing all your family could be there.
Lonely is having lost your mother and not really
    knowing what she was like when she was alive.

Lonely is not having someone to love
   and to have someone to love you back.
Lonely is really depressing.
Lonely is something I wish I wasn't.

Young or old—loneliness does not discriminate.

It is a college girl, sitting on her bed listening to the happy talk and laughter bursting up and down the halls outside her room as she bites her knuckles and cries in isolation. Shut out, she wonders, "Am I missing some important part in me that shows a person how to be happy?" Then self-estrangement comes and she finds herself playing with a razor blade.

It is a teenager looking for the end of life when he has only just begun to see his life begin.

Despair has many profiles.

It is a woman riddled with depression for seemingly no good reason.

"I don't know why I feel as awful as I do," she confesses, "I just do!" Years of tests and therapy and hundreds of opiates and treatments later, she still feels awful, and that awful, awful feeling leads her to despair.

Depression needs a reason to help work itself out, a valid core that, once recognized, can be dealt with and discarded. Having "no good reason," it links itself to guilt and self-deprecation that intensifies an already unbearable pain, and it becomes despair.

Another woman finds herself consumed with fear; she is exhausted night after sleepless night. Her eyes pop open once again at four in the morning, she looks at the person sleeping quietly beside her, and angry resentments ferment. She thinks of others—their peaceful sleep, their ability when they awake to get moving, to work, to play, to laugh, to relax—when all she has to look forward to is another day filled with anxiety that has no explanation.

Despair is broken hearts, broken dreams, broken promises, and many broken lives, but . . .

God uses broken things!

Looking through my kitchen window, over the sink which is so often the hub of snapped tensions, wrung hands, and mopped-up tears, one sees a huge acacia tree. It leans precariously downhill and would have toppled years ago had it not been for one bent bough— broken but not severed, fallen but still functional.

I well remember the storm that felled it.

There was a quiet the night before, an eerie stillness, and in the twilight several little birds (too dark to see just what they were) buzzed frantically around a large brown owl. He sat stoically on the top branch of an old dead fir. Suddenly he flew—an awesome sight. His great bulk pushed through the air dragging heavy on the flapping wings. It was a magnificent sight that made me hold my breath. He flew into the branches of the acacia tree.

The Santa Ana winds came up, sixty to eighty miles per hour, with a terrifying intensity that wreaked havoc through the canyon. We heard the roar swooping down upon us, and we cringed. It snapped the top off the old dead fir and sent it bouncing across the roof. Power lines were downed and we were plunged in darkness.

In the morning light we saw that the acacia was split, one huge bough broken and bent right over.

That broken bough took root and sent new shoots reaching upward. It has grown into a massive trunk that has become the prop, the stability, and the bulwark of the tilted tree.

God can take every aspect of our broken lives and root them in the soil of his strength. Like the broken bough pushing the fullness of its weight against the falling tree, our broken desolation can become instead the strength and steadying bulwark of our lives.

Once when I was feeling broken in spirit, a friend of mine sent me a prayer (Tagore paraphrased) that she had carefully written out in beautiful calligraphy, illustrated with vines, leaves, and flowers. I carry it in my Bible.

When my heart is hard and parched up, Oh my Lord, come upon me with a shower of mercy. When grace is lost from life, come with a burst of song. When I am shut out from beyond by a tumultuous clamor, come to me, Lord of silence, with your peace and rest. When my heart is crouched up in a corner and my mind blinded with delusion, come, come, with your shining light!

And because he is the Lord of hope, he comes.

Hope is a series of little victories coming from a big defeat.

It is a moving from, toward.

The "from" is from despair, the "toward" is toward the promise of another day.

It is a slow plodding, sometimes only creeping, but . . . going in the right direction.

God has promised to give us "strength for the *day*." He did not project a week, a month, or a year in advance, just one *day* strengthened one at a time. This we sometimes have to break down into strength for each painful minute, one following on the tail of another like a train of elephants, trunk to tail, tugging on each other.

Hope is a series of small steps, taken one at a time.

Amy Carmichael, the frail young woman who dedicated her life to bringing the hope of the love of Christ to the people of India (and who spent the last twenty years of her life completely bedridden and in constant pain), said that she learned the full meaning of the scripture, "Thy word is a lamp unto my feet and a light unto my path," while taking a series of small steps over the slippery rocks as she made her way up through a forest in the darkness of the night.

She had a lantern (lamp) which she had to hold very low to show her each step along the way. Unlike a large flashlight that would illuminate the path a long way ahead, a lantern throws out only just enough light for one small step . . . and then another . . . and another.

A friend of mine went through pernicious despair that ended in a nervous breakdown.

"I was laid so low," she said, "that even brushing my teeth each morning became an enormous act of courage!"

She came out of the experience riddled with the fear of people and public places.

"My head wobbles," she said, "like one of those little wooden Japanese dolls. If I don't walk very carefully I am afraid that it might come completely off!"

Encouraged to venture out alone, she decided to make her first foray to the local supermarket, a familiar place where the people knew her and she knew them. The important thing was not the act of shopping; it was to take that first brave step of going out on her own, milling about with people, and getting through the checkstand and back home.

Wound up tight in a bundle of anxiety, she rushed up and down the aisles, mechanically grabbing this and that to fill her cart with one thought racing through her mind, to get out of there as fast as possible. Halfway through she panicked.

"I suddenly went numb," she said. "My head came off!"

She left the cart with all its groceries standing in the middle of an aisle and fled, thoroughly defeated. It took her a week to get up enough nerve to try it again. This time she was wiser, smarter.

"I decided to take a smaller step," she said. "Instead of trying to fill my cart, I set as my goal the purchase of just four small items. It was quite easily done, and I slid through the checkstand, would you believe, smiling!"

Eleanor Roosevelt said, "You gain strength, courage, and confidence by every experience in which you really stop to look fear in the face. You are able to say to yourself, 'I lived through this horror. I can take the next thing that comes along.' . . . You must do the thing you think you cannot do."

For those living on the edge of tomorrow, the thing they think they "cannot do" may be something as small as four items slid through a checkstand.

Barbara Gordon, the author of *I'm Dancing As Fast*

As I Can, found her way back from the despair and devastation of mental illness. She says how wonderful it would be if our schools could teach courses in "starting over" to prepare us for moving through what she calls life's grimmest moments.

For example, she suggests that required for graduation would be a master class on "learning how to transform the screeching silence of loneliness into the spiritual serenity of solitude." The problem is, she says, it is unteachable!

We find our way back through many trials and errors. What works for some does not always work for others.

It would indeed be marvelous if there were pat answers that we could list all in a row: one, two, three, four, and however many (hundreds? thousands?) necessary to serve as a curriculum for complete recovery from almost everything. But there are no pat answers, not even from the Scriptures.

We have instead the promise of God's presence as our consolation and our strength and the lamp of God's promises as our daily hope. Held in the low places of our lives, it leads us through the darkness, step by step, to help us find our way.

It is only in the darkness that we can see the stars. In the darkness of our despair the promises of God become our stars of hope.

When I am crushed and teetering on the edge of despair, I take from the comfort of the Psalms, a star of hope. I personalize the pronouns: "God is *my* refuge and *my* strength, *my* very present help in time of trouble" (46:1). "No one (that means me) who trusts in the Lord shall ever be desolate" (34:22).

Bryan Jeffery Leech has written many beautiful hymns and musical compositions. While browsing through the hymnal one Sunday morning as I waited for the service to begin, I came across a beautiful prayer of his that has come to mean a great deal in my life: "Father, during this coming week there may be times when I shall not be able to sense Your presence or to be aware of Your nearness. When I am lonely and by myself, I *trust* you to be my companion. When I am depressed and anxious, I *trust* you to lift my spirits. When I forget you, I *trust* that you will never forget me" (excerpts from "A Pledge of Trust").

Trust is the bulwark of our hope.

I once visited a woman deep in despair. She was lying flat out on her bed. She had pinned a note to her pillow, "No one understands." I quietly took out my marking pen and wrote, "Oh yes someone does." I opened my Bible to the book of Psalms. "O Lord you have examined my heart and know everything about me . . . you know my every thought . . . " and I went on to read her all of Psalm 139.

And then I shared with her Psalm 40: "He lifted me out of the pit of despair . . . and set my feet on a hard, firm path and steadied me as I walked along. He has given me a new song to sing of praises to our God. Now many will hear of the glorious things he did for me and stand in awe before the Lord and put their trust in him" (*Living Bible*).

Although we have no pat answers, we can offer the reflection of the light and shadows of our own broken experiences as a gift of hope one to another. "This helps me, maybe it will help you too."

The prayers I pray for those plunged into the pit of

despair are not for huge, whomping, all-at-once solutions, but rather for day-to-day encouragements. "Send her something, Lord, to encourage her heart today."

These simple prayers God, in his kind mercy, sometimes answers in the strangest ways.

One woman phoned me nearly every morning for a month. She was going downhill from depression into a deep despair and since she was in a position where she could not even "come on in and sit a while and talk," I offered her the lifeline of the telephone. I made myself available to pray with her and, of course, recommended that she seek professional help. Before she called each day she was to try and find a brightness that we could focus on, a star shining through the darkness of her despair.

She called one morning, sneezing and blowing her nose frantically in the middle of a horrid cold.

"The only good thing I can see in today," she said, "is that the new soft paper towels my husband brought home with the groceries last night make better cold tissues than the small blow-your-nose-once-then-throw-it-away regular brands!"

"Great!" I laughed. "Why don't you take a minute and write and tell the manufacturer that!"

She did.

"I wrote not only to the paper towel company," she said, "but I wrote to the manufacturers of many of the other products in my cupboards that I have used for years, taken for granted, enjoyed, found good, and never thanked them for!"

She went on a letter writing jag that became for her the best of therapies, and I am sure there were many public relations departments delighted to get commendations on their products. It was a small, seemingly insignificant step that helped pull her into positive thought patterns, followed by positive action.

Hope is the resilience of the human spirit that says I can and will come back!

The greatest hope for despair that the world has ever known came wrapped in swaddling clothes, lying in a manger.

In our home we keep the hope of Christmas visible and alive throughout the house the year around. We are a family that live and breathe tradition. We bake the heart-shaped cookies, color the eggs, carve the pumpkin, dress the turkey, and, most of all, we glory in the glory that is Christmastime.

From the time that they were born the children loved the wonder of the Christmas tree. Through the years we have developed a tradition of trimming the tree with handmade ornaments brought by little friends (the friends have now grown big, but they still want to make and bring their ornaments!). These are carefully packed away and pulled out again year after year as treasured tokens of friendships that we cherish and hope will last a lifetime through.

We each have our favorites. I have a smiling Grinch (making his topsy-turvy world right again, with hope renewed) painted by an artist friend. He goes on a middle branch, up front. The little angel in a crib, guarded by a mother and a father acorn bird, goes to the right and down low so children can both see and touch. We have high-up ornaments, low-down unbreakable ornaments, ornaments to be used as toys to be given to children who may come to visit for whom we do not have a gift . . .

Taking down the tree was always doom and gloom with tears of disappointment, so we thought up a new tradition. Each of us chooses a favorite ornament to hang about the house, anywhere we please, that we leave up the year around. These are the first off the tree and the first to be put back on. It reminds us that Christmas is never ever really past, and it keeps the hope of Christmas alive and visible daily in all our lives.

So if you come to visit us at any time at all, you will see hanging on the chandelier in the dining-room, reflecting the brilliance of a thousand lights, a golden snowflake, twirling *joy* from a bit of thread.

On the door knob of the bathroom is a stuffed calico dove—*peace* purchased from a church bazaar. His wings are droopy now, so that he looks more like a seal with flippers flapping, and every time I take a bath I remind myself that I really must take a stitch here and there to perk him up, but then I never do!

Our daughter chose a stained glass heart inscribed, "*Love* makes all things beautiful."

The ornaments we choose may change from year to year, but there is one that never changes. It hangs in the place of honor and has the greatest visibility— the entry hall—for everyone to see as they come in and out. It is a little wooden ornament carved around a child lying in a bed of straw. Above him is a shining star, it's brightness is greater than the deepest darkness, and the light coming from that star fills our hearts with the presence of Christ always with us, he who is our *hope*.